# SCOTCH WHISKY

*"To Elsa, Flora, Chloe, Molly and especially Kitty"*

AUTHOR'S ACKNOWLEDGMENTS

*I woud like to thank the following people: Geraldine Coates, Charlie Maclean, Dave Broom, Gavin Smith, Rosemary Gallacher, Christine McCafferty and the late Michael Jackson. I would also like to thank the long-suffering staff at Carlton Books, not least my editor: Martin Corteel.*

First published in 2015 as *The Treasures of Scotch Whisky*
Reissued in 2017 as *The Story of Scotch Whisky*

This revised edition published in 2018 by
Carlton Books Limited
20 Mortimer Street
London W1T 3JW

A CIP catalogue for this book is available from the British Library

Editorial Manager: Martin Corteel
Design Manager: Luke Griffin
Design: Harj Ghundale
Picture Research: Paul Langan
Production: Lisa Cook

ISBN: 978 1 78739 149 9

Printed and bound in China

# SCOTCH WHISKY

### The Essential Guide for Single Malt Lovers

Tom Bruce-Gardyne

CARLTON BOOKS

# CONTENTS

# INTRODUCTION

Unlike many drinks, there is no **instant gratification with Scotch whisky. Few if any of us were smitten by our first sip, and the sweetness often there on the nose can be hard to find on the tongue. To the uninitiated, there is something almost primal about single malts with their raw, pungent, bittersweet character and that's true of many blends, too. But as whisky lovers know, it is worth persevering until you are well and truly seduced by this strange brew.**

The story of Scotland's national drink is equally compelling, and goes back hundreds of years. While the first recorded mention of whisky is from the late fifteenth century, its origins are older still, and it is tempting to believe it was at least partly born of necessity. As well as being a drink to share, whisky was something to rub on aching joints, cleanse wounds, act as an antibiotic and numb the pain of a long, Scottish winter. Was the water of life discovered by accident by the Scots, or did those Irish monks bring more than Christianity with them in their coracles ... who knows?

This book takes you on a journey through whisky's evolution from a wild, spirit hot from the still to modern-day drink mellowed in wood. We consider the production process and ponder how a few humble ingredients – water, malted barley and a sprinkling of yeast – in the case of malts, can produce something so infinitely diverse and complex. Then it visits the whisky regions to see how each developed its own identity, before touring key malt distilleries.

The third part of the book explores how whisky has soaked its way into popular culture through books, films and music hall. Scotch added true grit to countless pulp fiction heroes and an air of sophistication to Hollywood stars who in turn helped promote it to a wider audience. It also seeped into the poetry of Robert Burns, who happily confessed it to be his muse and appreciated its earthy charms, perhaps better than anyone, so it is only fitting that Burns Night should be a raucous, whisky-fuelled celebration of his life.

*Scotch Whisky* celebrates this beguiling spirit in images as much as words. With a colourful past stretching back over five centuries, there is a rich archive to plunder and reproduce to bring the story alive. All that is missing is one vital ingredient, but you can rectify that yourself. With a freshly poured dram in one hand and this book in the other, hopefully you will be in for a treat.

*Tom Bruce-Gardyne,*
*Edinburgh, February 2018*

# HOW WHISKY IS MADE

To make whisky you first have to make beer, and any distillery visit will lead you by the nose from the beery aromas of a brewery to the sweet scent of distillation. But before that you will learn about the ingredients, starting with water, which is used to steep the barley, make the mash, condense the spirit and reduce its strength for maturation and again at the time of bottling unless it is a cask-strength whisky. Without water there would be no water of life, yet whether it is hard or soft, tinged with peat or crystal clear, its impact on flavour is marginal.

For malt whisky the grain is always barley, much of it from Scotland's East Coast barley belt that runs from the Black Isle to the Borders. The whisky industry uses various strains of barley, but the choice is more about maximizing alcoholic yield than influencing taste. First the grain is plunged into a cold bath where it doubles in size, and traditionally it was then spread out on a stone malting floor for a week as it began to sprout little rootlets and begin germinating. The grain had to be turned twice a day by men with wooden shovels to prevent it matting together. Today, apart from a few distilleries like Bowmore and Highland Park, the process is done entirely by industrial maltings. What remains critical, however, is whether the kilns to dry the grain use peat or not. Peat is partially decomposed vegetable matter – grass, heather, gorse and the like, that has been slowly compacted into a hard black layer over thousands of years. Only when lit does it release its pungent, bittersweet aroma that seeps into the malted barley as its blue smoke wafts up from the kiln. By mixing the ratio of peated to unpeated malt, the distiller can determine the peatiness, or phenolic content, of the finished whisky.

The malt is ground to a coarse grist and mixed with hot water in a large, circular mash-tun with rotating rakes to prevent it clogging. The aim is to extract all the soluble sugars, and three separate mashes are needed, each one progressively hotter. What is left is compressed into cattle cake, while the liquid is drained off into large wooden vessels called washbacks, having been injected with yeast. Here it ferments to a cloudy brew of around 8 per cent alcohol that some of the more hardened distillery workers used to drink by the pint. The wash, as it is now called, is filled into a wash still – basically a towering copper kettle – and heated for a first distillation. The component parts of the wash are teased apart thanks to their different boiling points. The wash still takes the alcoholic strength to around 21 per cent, which is then trebled in a second distillation in the spirit still. If you are Irish, or that way inclined, you would distil it a third time to produce a slightly lighter spirit, though twice is enough for most Scots. Stills have always been made of copper, which reacts with the boiling liquid and helps strip out some of the impurities. The more copper contact as the vapours rise up the still and then condense back down, the cleaner the spirit will be. This explains why the shape of the still and rate of distillation help to make every single malt unique.

The vapours that make it over the top of the still then travel down the copper pipe known as the lyne arm to be condensed, either in a modern condenser or an old-fashioned worm tub. The liquid then flows through the spirit safe, a glass-fronted box of polished brass. The stillman rejects the volatile alcohols, or foreshots, until the spirit is deemed worth collecting. Half an hour later, as the strength slowly falls, the feints appear and these too are rejected. The middle part, or cut, is the new-

LEFT Crystal clear newmake spirit flows through the spirits safe at Laphroaig on Islay.

make spirit and represents a balance of clean alcohols and impurities. Though toxic in a higher dose these impurities, or congeners, give a whisky its distillery character and add an extra kick to any resulting hangover.

Most distillery tours end with a dram and a visit to the distillery shop, with perhaps a cursory glimpse at a warehouse. Slumbering in the dark, row upon row of casks seem to be doing not very much at all, yet it is here where the real magic occurs. A clear, raw spirit is transformed over the years into a mellow golden whisky, picking up colour as well as certain flavours from the oak. Breathing in air and exhaling alcohol through the pores in the wood, the whisky loses its rough edges and gains complexity in a way that's still not fully understood. Maturation may be the most mystical and uncontrollable part of the process, but it determines perhaps two-thirds of a whisky's character.

The rules on maturation – at least three years in an oak cask – only came in a century ago, and prior to that most whisky would have been a rough, immature spirit. There was little incentive for prolonged ageing with whisky losing up to two per cent a year in evaporation – the so-called "angels' share". The industry relied on second-hand European oak wine barrels, particularly sherry casks which were plentiful given the drink's popularity and the fact it was nearly all shipped in bulk. Gradually sherry casks have been replaced by American oak ex-bourbon barrels that now account for 90 per cent of the industry's needs. A first-fill sherry butt (500 litres) will give the whisky a spicy, resinous fruitcake character, compared to the sweeter coconut and vanilla notes of its bourbon equivalent at half the size. As of 2015 the former cost from €750 (£550), compared to US$130 (£85) for the latter. The type of oak, whether American or European, the previous contents, the length of maturation and whether the cask is a "first-fill" (i.e. never previously used for Scotch) all play a part. A first-fill cask will imbue more colour and flavour in five years than a third-fill in twenty or thirty.

OPPOSITE Pot stills come in almost as many shapes as there are distilleries. This determines the amount of copper contact during distillation which in turn will influence the purity and flavour of the spirit.

PART ONE

# THE HISTORY OF SCOTCH WHISKY

# MONKS AND FRIARS

When, some twenty years ago, the Scotch whisky industry celebrated its five hundredth anniversary, it traced its birth to a terse note in the Exchequer Rolls of 1494: "To Friar John Cor, by order of the King, to make acqua vitae VIII bolls of malt." The friar from Lindores Abbey in Fife was clearly distilling on some scale. Eight bolls of malt would make you more than a few hundred bottles of Scotch whisky today.

This may be the first recorded mention of *aqua vitae*, the water of life, but as the whisky writer Charles Maclean says, "it raises as many questions as it answers". It tells us that by the end of the fifteenth century distillation had reached Scotland, but not when it began, nor whether it was being drunk, used in medicine or perfume, or even gunpowder. The history of whisky as we know it might be younger than we thought; or, more likely, considerably older.

The secret of distillation spread from Ancient China via India and the Middle East. By the fourth century BC, Aristotle was distilling water by boiling sea water

RIGHT The ruins of Lindores Abbey in Fife and spiritual home of Scotch whisky where Friar John Cor was granted the right to make aqua vitae in 1494. The abbey was sacked in 1559 at the behest of John Knox.

and collecting the steam in balls of wool suspended above it. It was hardly alcohol, but it shared the same principle of applying heat to a body or mass in order to release its essence or "spirit", which would then condense back into a purified form. The discovery of distillation also mirrored the alchemists' quest for the mythical quintessence that could transform base metal into gold – an obvious fascination for a man like King James IV, who was deeply into science and often deeply in debt.

While the light of knowledge from Arab and Greek scholars was mostly snuffed out during the Dark Ages, it flickered on in Irish monasteries. It is therefore tempting to believe that Irish monks brought more than Christianity with them when they sailed across to Scotland in their coracles. The McBeatha family from Ireland may well have known the secret when they became the hereditary physicians to the Lord of the Isles in around 1300.

Then again, perhaps whisky was simply discovered by accident by the Scots themselves. Beer had been brewed in Scotland since neolithic times, and whisky is nothing if not distilled beer. Perhaps, in an effort to rescue some heather ale that had turned sour, someone decided to boil it up. Maybe a few droplets of vapour condensed to give a glimpse of what became the national spirit?

BELOW King James I of England (and James VI of Scotland) battled to impose his will on the wild and intemperate Western Isles through the Statutes of Iona in 1609.

## MAKING MEN MERRY

Whenever it happened, the secret of this magic brew soon spread. It was certainly a wonder drug in the view of Peter Morwyng, who wrote one of the first books on distilling in 1559. Besides being a cure for tired eyes, palsy, poor memory, ringworm and spots, he decreed: "It is mervelous profitable for frantic man and such as be melancholy ... It taketh away sadness, pensiveness; it maketh men merri, witti and encreaseth audacitie."

By 1579 distilling had become sufficiently mainstream to provoke fears of a grain shortage. That year an Act of the Scottish Parliament restricted the practice to "Earls, Lords, Barons and Gentlemen for their own use". In 1609 James VI of Scotland (James I of England) attempted to impose order on the Western Isles through the Statutes of Iona, which shows how whisky was becoming a commercial trade. It blamed "the great poverty of the isles" on people's "inordinate love of strong wines and acquavite, which they purchased partly from dealers among themselves, [and] partly from merchants belonging to the mainland". Unless they happened to be "barons or wealthy gentlemen", they were ordered to rely on their own stills and not buy from the mainland.

The fear of the chaos unleashed by "strong wines and acquavite", and the desire to control and tax them, became a common refrain of government. In 1644 the first excise duty was imposed, and though a temporary tax it was not long before the State became used to this sweet source of revenue. Within 20 years, the first "gaugers" (excisemen) had appeared on the scene, with the power to

**BELOW** This extract from "Canedolia" by the late poet, Edwin Morgan, is carved into the wall of the Scottish Parliament in Edinburgh. "A wee ferintosh" refers to what was Scotland's oldest commercial distillery on the Black Isle.

**BELOW RIGHT** The secret of distillation spread from Ancient China via India and the Middle East. By the fourth century BC, it had reached Ancient Greece.

tell us about
last night
well, we had
a wee ferintosh
and we lay
on the quirding.
it was pure
strontian!

Edwin
Morgan

enter any "distilling house" and collect duty. Meanwhile explorers to the far-flung reaches of the Highlands and Islands reported back with awe at the strength and quantity of spirits consumed. Visiting Mull, Martin Martin wrote that "the natives are accustomed to take a large dose of acquavite as a corrective against the climate" – a tradition that doubtless continues.

On the Black Isle at Ferintosh, near Dingwall, Duncan Forbes III was Scotland's first known commercial distiller. The scale of production can be gauged from his massive £54,000 bid for compensation when the Jacobites burned down "his brewery of acqua vitae" in 1689. Instead of paying, the Scottish Parliament offered him virtually tax-free distilling so long as he used grain from his own land. The Forbes family extended their estate, built three distilleries and were making profits of over £2 million by 1784 when the State finally ended the concession. By then, it is said, Ferintosh accounted for almost two-thirds of all the legal whisky in Scotland, and it was clearly a serious brand, for its passing was mourned by Robert Burns, who penned the lines: "Thee Ferintosh! O sadly lost! Scotland lament frae coast to coast!"

## WHAT IS THIS … WHISKY?

It was not until the 1730s that we find mention of "whiskie". One of the earliest references was a letter from Bailie John Steuart of Inverness to his brother-in-law urging him to "keep a sober regular dyet" and "forbear drinking that poisonous drink, I mean drams of brandie and whiskie". The word was a corruption of uiskie or uisge beatha – the Scots Gaelic translation of aqua vitae, the water of life.

The word "Usquebaugh" appears in Dr Johnson's famous dictionary of 1755 with the following definition: "It is a compounded distilled spirit, being drawn on aromaticks; and the Irish sort is particularly distinguished for its pleasant and mild flavour. The Highland sort is somewhat hotter; and, by corruption, in Scottish they call it whisky."

# UNION, REVOLT ... AND EXCISE

When the Union between England and Scotland was formed in 1707, funds were needed urgently to pay for it, and a key source of revenue was to be the taxation of drink.

**BELOW** The Battle of Culloden of 1746 crushed the second Jacobite uprising under Charles Edward Stuart, "Bonnie Prince Charlie". The brutal repression of Highland culture that followed, including the banning of kilts and bagpipes, helped turn whisky into the spirit of defiance.

At first the Hanoverian regime trod extremely carefully, as though sensing trouble. A Board of Excise was set up in Edinburgh, but it was not until 10 years after successfully crushing the first Jacobite revolt in 1715 that the authorities dared to double the tax on malt. Although it was still only half that of England, it provoked a brewery strike in Edinburgh and a full-scale riot in Glasgow that left 11 dead and the house of Daniel Campbell, the city's MP, burned to the ground. With the £6,000 he was paid in compensation, Campbell bought Islay and played a key role in developing distilling on the island.

The Malt Tax of 1725 hit beer harder than whisky, which in those days would have been a very inconsistent spirit to say the least. It was seldom, if ever, allowed to mellow in wood, and would have been drunk raw and almost hot from the still. No wonder it was often compounded with heather, herbs, wild berries and honey to help it slip down. It was around this time that the first licensed distillers began to crop up in the Lowlands, among them John Stein at Kennetpans in Clackmannanshire.

Stein had four sons who all became distillers and a daughter who married John Haig – another whisky dynasty. Together with a third distilling family, the Phelpses, they came to represent whisky's industrial revolution and were to some extent a Lowland mafia compared to their rustic Highland cousins. The Steins' Kilbagie distillery was the biggest in Scotland when it was built in the 1770s and had a workforce of over 300. It produced so much draff from the distilling process that it was said to feed 7,000 black cattle and 2,000 sheep.

## CROSSING THE LINE

After the Battle of Culloden in 1746, when the second Jacobite rebellion was crushed, the government banned bagpipes and the wearing of tartan.

LEFT "The Illicit Highland Whisky Still" by Edwin Landseer (c.1829) is a classic, romanticized depiction of whisky. The Highlander in his bothey astride a dead stag with his bare-footed bairns, and a small, copper still bubbling away in the background.

This deliberate attack on Highland culture only added to the allure of whisky, whose production grew with each attempt to tax and control it. As the Irish said of poteen, illicit Scotch was: "superior in sweetness, salubriety and gusto to all that machinery, science and capital can produce in the legalized way".

By 1760 it was claimed that licensed distilleries accounted for only a tenth of all the whisky drunk in Scotland. The rest came from private stills which gurgled away in every corner of the country from the furthest-flung farmstead to the city centre. In Edinburgh it was said there were 400 stills of which only eight were licensed. There had always been smuggling, but it began to surge after a series of disastrous harvests prompted a ban on distilling in 1756.

A further run of poor harvests in the 1780s highlighted the tension between feeding the masses and supplying an increasingly voracious whisky industry. When the mob turned up at James Haig's Edinburgh distillery of Canonmills, he had to assure them he was not storing any carrots, turnips or peas to make his whisky. Meanwhile the government finally banned private stills, though probably to little effect, and brought in new laws that split the country in two when it came to whisky.

The Wash Act of 1784 allowed distillers north of a line from the Firth of Clyde to the Firth of Tay to use much smaller stills and pay less tax than Lowland distillers, who were naturally upset. The fact that Highland whisky was theoretically banned south of the line was little consolation given the scale of smuggling that was going on. Indeed, because the new tax regime encouraged those in the Lowlands to run their large, flat-bottomed stills ever faster, demand for the somewhat gentler Highland whisky only increased.

Lowland stills were being worked at ferocious speed, with all manner of ugly flavours and impurities finding their way into the finished drink. By the late 1770s, the Steins had discovered a whole new market in England – not for whisky, but for raw spirit that was rectified into gin. In just five years this trade jumped from 2,000 to

184,000 gallons, prompting a vicious price war with the London distillers who successfully lobbied Westminster to ramp up the duty on Scottish spirit. When the Lowland distillers were then told to give 12 months' notice of intent to export, the Haig–Stein empire collapsed with massive debts. In time the two families recovered and rose again with the advent of continuous distillation in the 1820s.

By 1800 four-fifths of legal Scotch whisky came from the Lowlands, from 31 licensed distilleries, almost half the number in the Highlands which tended to be much smaller. Below the surface the trade in illicit whisky began to surge, encouraged by periodic bans on distilling and by every tax increase. It was smuggled southwards along the old drove roads used for taking cattle from upland pastures to be sold in the big markets like Falkirk. Facing the smugglers was a thinly stretched, hopelessly outnumbered body of excisemen, or gaugers. It was an unequal battle, as Thomas Guthrie, minister of Brechin in Angus, makes clear in his account (below) of smugglers coming to town.

**ABOVE** John Murdoch (1818–1903), former exciseman turned newspaper owner and campaigner for crofter's rights.

"They were often caught, no doubt, with the contraband whisky in their possession. Then they were subjected to heavy fines besides the loss of their goods. But – daring, stout, active fellows – they often broke through the nets ... I have seen a troop of thirty of them riding Indian file, and in broad day, through the streets of Brechin, after they had succeeded in disposing of their whisky, and, as they rode leisurely along, beating time with their formidable cudgels on the empty barrels to the great amusement of the public and mortification of the excisemen ... Everybody, with few exceptions, drank what was in reality illicit whisky – far superior to that made under the eye of the Excise – lords and lairds, members of parliament and ministers of the Gospel, and everybody else."

# LEGISLATION AND ROYAL PATRONAGE

By 1822 there was even a name for illicit Scotch. It was called Glenlivet – a regional style of whisky demanded by the King himself when he descended on Scotland that year.

George IV's visit, masterminded by that bestselling author and consummate PR man, Walter Scott, was a big deal. It was the first time a reigning monarch had set foot north of the border since 1650. As for the whisky, it could have come from over 200 illicit stills said to be operating in this remote corner of Upper Speyside.

Despite enjoying royal patronage, the tide of opinion was beginning to turn against illicit whisky, at least among the landowners who were faced with tougher fines if their tenants were caught operating an unlicensed still. There was also a growing fear of anarchy if people so routinely flouted the law. Yet much more important in persuading illicit whisky makers to come in from the cold was the relaxation of the rules and a lowering of the fees. By halving the duty on spirit, and setting the licence at a modest £10, the Excise Act of 1823 became the midwife to the modern whisky industry.

RIGHT King George IV's "Northern excursion" of 1822, the first time a reigning monarch had visited Scotland since 1650, and the tartan fest that ensued, inspired much satire. It was noted the King, dubbed "the portly Hanoverian", wore flesh-coloured tights beneath his kilt to conceal his gouty legs.

A Thousand Warm receptions in the North.

The trickle of distillers who had previously been taking out licences turned into a spate that year as dozens followed suit. Not that every former smuggler decided to give up, and there were tales of distilleries like Lochnagar on Deeside being torched, and of distillers being attacked. Glenlivet's founder, George Smith – the first man to take out a licence in the glen – was confronted by a smuggling gang at an inn near Glenshee. According to legend, the ringleader burst into his room and threatened to disembowel him on the spot. Quick as a flash, Smith whipped out a pair of pistols from under the bed sheets, and held one to the man's head and fired the other up the chimney with a deafening blast.

Within five years of the Act, whisky production had trebled to an estimated 10 million gallons, while Campbeltown in deepest Argyll witnessed the industry's first boom with no fewer than 27 distilleries built between 1823 and 1837. Of course all of them were malt distilleries relying on old-fashioned pot stills which, then as now, had to be filled and emptied with each batch. Having done this with the wash still, you have to repeat the process with the spirit still to achieve the double distillation you need for Scotch.

## SCOTCH BLENDS IN

Once there was grain and malt whisky to marry together, blended Scotch was an accident waiting to happen. However the early blenders stuck to mixing malts for a few decades yet, which gives the lie to a fair number of famous brands. Johnnie Walker may still be going strong, but it wasn't born in 1820. The father of blended whisky is said to be Andrew Usher, whose family-

BELOW What more did a captain in the Royal Navy need when at sea than a case of Andrew Usher's pioneering brand of Old Vatted Glenlivet?

owned drinks business in Edinburgh happened to be agents for Glenlivet on Speyside. Usher began mixing the malts to produce Old Vatted Glenlivet – known as OVG, and once the Spirits Act of 1860 allowed people to blend whiskies from different distilleries before duty was paid, he began adding grain whisky. The result was smoother, more rounded and cheaper to produce. In a few years he released the first true commercial blended Scotch – Usher's Green Stripe, which was soon flattered by imitation. Many of the early blends were cooked up by grocers like John Walker & Sons of Kilmarnock and Chivas Brothers in Aberdeen.

For all the romance of Highland whisky, with its slow pot stills bubbling away in remote glens, it was the big city blenders who cajoled the malt distillers to up their game and produce a consistent, quality spirit. The blends they produced had to compete with popular, triple-distilled Irish whiskies, and convince the English bourgeoisie that Scotch had a place in their drinks cupboard. What was perceived as a crude, outdoor spirit, suitable for the grouse moor or river bank, craved the same social acceptance as brandy and soda.

Help was at hand from an unlikely source. A microscopic aphid called phylloxera with an insatiable appetite for vine roots was first spotted in France in 1863. Before long it was munching its way through swathes of vineyards, including those of Cognac. As

RIGHT An early diagram of a continuous still showing the two columns. The wash enters the rectifier on the right where the perforated copper plates strip out the heavier compounds and is then vaporized in the second column, or analyser, on the left.

prices soared, unscrupulous merchants began passing off cheaper brandies, before faking the spirit altogether. Cognac's reputation was badly dented, and Scotch seized its opportunity with both hands to present a credible alternative. Society magazines were blitzed with adverts featuring upper-crust types drinking whisky and soda in their London clubs. There were also frequent references to Highlanders, though copywriters appeared confused as to whether to portray them as noble warriors or comic drunks.

## THE CONTINUOUS STILL

For a Scotsman in a hurry like Robert Stein, the plodding production of pot stills was completely out of step with the industrial revolution. Distilling's holy grail would be a still that could convert the wash into spirit in a continuous flow, and various prototypes were tested out by distillers on the Continent and in Ireland. Stein produced his "patent still" in 1828 and installed it at Cameronbridge distillery in Fife. The wash was heated and then sprayed into various chambers in a column separated by cloths. It certainly produced spirit, though how good it was is unclear. Despite Stein's best efforts, no other distiller was tempted to buy a patent still.

One man who did see the potential was Aeneas Coffey, who had retired from running Ireland's Excise to do a spot of distilling by himself in Dublin. This ultimate gamekeeper turned poacher gave the world the Coffey still in 1830, and after a few modifications involving copper plates within the metal columns, it became the standard continuous still. The history of whisky could have been very different had the Irish distillers not turned their noses up at his invention, causing Coffey to move to London in 1840. By then his stills were starting to appear in Scotland's new grain distilleries in the Lowlands. Before long they were pumping out a much blander, smoother spirit at up to 85 per cent alcohol by volume. By the mid-nineteenth century they were producing more alcohol than pot stills in Scotland and England, though not in Ireland.

# THE WHISKY BARONS

John Dewar and his younger brother Tommy Dewar turned a local whisky business in Perth into a global giant thanks to Dewar's White Label.

The blend, now owned by Bacardi, sells around 3 million cases worldwide and claims to be America's favourite brand of Scotch. Back in 1880, when the Dewar brothers inherited the firm, annual profits were just £1,231, and the prospects weren't encouraging. When Tommy Dewar arrived in London, aged 21, "to wake up the south", he discovered that one of his leads was dead and the other bankrupt.

**BELOW** Tommy Dewar, the quintessential "Scotsman on the make", launched the Dewar's White Label brand and helped it become one of the world's biggest-selling blends. He was also an MP, then member of the House of Lords, and died a multi-millionaire.

In 1892 he set sail aboard the *City of Paris* and returned, two years later, having visited 26 countries and appointed 32 agents. Though the venture cost a staggering sum, no one minded, for orders were flooding in from Canada and the United States. A second sales trip took him as far as New Zealand, spreading the gospel of Dewar's White Label.

Tommy understood the power of advertising better than almost anyone, and in 1895 launched "the whisky of his forefathers" – a near 40-year campaign that included one of the first ever film commercials in 1897. A few years later, beside the Thames, next to the firm's bottling halls, a 200-foot illuminated Scotsman appeared; his kilt appeared to sway in the breeze as his arm repeatedly raised a glass of Dewar's Meanwhile Tommy drove around Britain's in the country's third-ever motorcar and became a fully-fledged member of the Establishment, rubbing shoulders with Edward VII. He entered politics, became Conservative MP for Tower Hamlets until being swept aside by the Liberals. In 1915 John Dewar & Sons decided to merge with arch-rival Buchanan's, which together were soon part of Distillers (DCL). Both brothers became barons and died in the winter of 1929, each leaving estates worth £5 million – or £270 million in today's money.

## PETER MACKIE

According Sir Robert Bruce Lockhart, *Peter Mackie* was: "one third genius, one third megalomaniac and one third eccentric." Born in 1855, he began working for his uncle's whisky business in Glasgow. As agents for Lagavulin and Laphroaig, he was sent to Islay, where he developed a real fondness for the island's whiskies. Of all the whisky barons, Mackie was the most attached to malt whisky, though his fortune came from his White Horse blend.

Named after Edinburgh's White Horse Inn, it was launched in 1901 as "a brand of the highest age and quality, second to nothing that has ever been offered the public". The public appeared unimpressed and Mackie conceded that White Horse required promotion. By 1914 he had spent £90,000 on advertising.

As a Tory, he loathed the Liberal, temperance-leaning Chancellor David Lloyd George, who raised spirits duty by a third in 1909. He believed the answer to alcohol's harm lay in maturation, saying: "Experience teaches us that the riotous and obstreperous conduct of drunks come from the young, fiery spirit which is sold, while men who may over-indulge in old matured whisky become sleepy and stupid, but not in a fighting mood." The minimum three-year maturation for Scotch whisky finally became law in 1916.

By then, White Horse exports had increased five-fold to 190,000 cases from 1900. With its heart of Lagavulin, it was the star performer among his blends that included the 18 year-old Logan's Perfection among others. On Islay, Mackie fell out with the Johnstones, who owned Laphroaig, and at one point ordered the distillery's water supply to be cut off. After the ensuing court case, he built the Malt Mill distillery beside Lagavulin to produce a carbon copy of Laphroaig. He failed in that endeavour, and died in 1924, three years before DCL swallowed his firm.

### JAMES BUCHANAN

*James Buchanan* was the quintessential whisky baron who rode the late Victorian whisky boom with panache. With his black silk top hat and monocle, he embodied the smooth sophistication that blended Scotch aspired to, in contrast to that raw Highland spirit – malt whisky. Born in Brockville, Ontario, in 1849, Buchanan returned to Scotland and joined his grain merchant brother in Glasgow – and, through grain, entered the whisky trade to become London agent for Charles Mackinlay & Co. aged 30. Five years later, backed by Glasgow blenders WP Lowrie, he created the Buchanan blend.

He felt the robust flavours of Scottish single malts would never appeal over the smoother, triple-distilled taste of Irish whiskey. His Buchanan's Blend was on the market by 1885 and describing itself as a mix of "Fine old Scotch whiskies" and "Suitable either for Grog or Toddy". With its white label on a dark bottle, it became known as Black & White – the name it eventually adopted as a brand.

Buchanan was a consummate salesman who became a "sole supplier" to the House of Commons in 1888, and soon after secured a Royal Warrant from Queen Victoria and Edward, Prince of Wales. In 1903, the company became James Buchanan & Co Ltd with a Scots Baronial HQ in London, complete with crenulations and turrets. Buchanan himself took to riding around in a horse-drawn buggy with a liveried footman to promote his whisky which had become Britain's top-selling blend by 1907.

Buchanan proposed a merger with his biggest rivals in 1909; it became Buchanan Dewar Ltd in 1919. Buchanan Dewar Ltd merged with John Walker & Sons in 1925 – as the Distillers Company. Buchanan was now Baron Woolavington, with properties in Sussex, Argentina and Kenya. He died in 1935, leaving an estate worth £7 million.

### JOHNNIE WALKER

"Born 1820 – still going strong" is the strapline of the world's best-selling Scotch whisky. They year may have

**ABOVE** Sir James Buchanan, Dewar's arch-rival and another natural-born salesman, launched the Buchanan's blend and Black & White. Eventually the two companies merged to form Buchanan Dewar Ltd, while Buchanan himself went on to become Lord Woolavington.

been when *Johnnie Walker*, aged 15, opened his grocery shop in Kilmarnock, but the whiskies came later. Diageo, its current owner, claims that Walker blended malt whiskies in his shop having learned the skill from blending tea, though there is a slight dearth of evidence. What is known is that it was not until after his death in 1857, that his son Alexander Walker produced Walker's Old Highland whisky – the first commercially available blend. He introduced the famous square bottle and slanting label, though it was the next generation – George and Alexander Walker and the firm's MD, James Stevenson – who really created the brand. They registered Johnnie Walker Red and Black Label in 1909, together with a short-lived White Label that was withdrawn when Dewar's complained.

The striding man logo, sketched on a napkin over lunch by the illustrator Tom Browne in 1908, was definitely more lion tamer than Scottish grocer. Had he been spotted on the streets of Kilmarnock in 1820, people would have assumed the circus was in town. Nevertheless, as a brand icon he certainly stood out from the sea of tartan that dominated whisky marketing at the time. By 1920 – before Coca-Cola had even crossed the Atlantic – Johnnie Walker whisky claimed to have 120 foreign markets.

*Chivas Regal* was also registered in 1909 as the flagship blend of the Chivas Brothers grocery store in Aberdeen – a grand emporium that stocked everything from "curious brandies" to "sperm candles". The store secured a royal warrant from Queen Victoria in 1843, two years before she bought Balmoral. Before long the brothers were blending whiskies in the basement, reserving the oldest and best malts for Chivas Regal.

In 1949 Sam Bronfman, head of Seagram's, bought Chivas Brothers for £85,000. The grandeur of the name appealed to Bronfman, who in later years was said to crave a knighthood that never came. "It was Mr. Sam's intention to make Chivas Regal the greatest name in Scotch whisky," a colleague later recalled. "This was not just a man marketing a new product – it was an artist producing his *chef d'oeuvre*." By the 1960s Seagram's had turned Chivas Regal 12-year-old into a powerhouse brand.

**BOTTOM** Named after a famous Clyde-built clipper that was in turn named after the witch in Burns's poem "Tam o' Shanter", Cutty Sark the blended Scotch whisky was born in 1923.

**BELOW** Johnnie Walker's iconic striding man dates from 1908 and is said to enjoy the same brand recognition as Coca-Cola.

# WHISKY AND THE BRITISH EMPIRE

With cognac in crisis, distilleries in Scotland and Ireland began to realize the world was up for grabs, starting with England. For most of the Victorian whisky boom the smart money was on the Irish.

When the Distillers Company (DCL) built Dublin's Phoenix Park distillery in 1878, it claimed that demand for Irish "whiskey" was five times greater than for Scotch. With its smooth, pot still taste, it was considered superior to the rougher, often un-aged blends coming from Scotland. Not that the Scots were above blurring the lines between the two styles. The giant Caledonian distillery, one of the biggest in Scotland, was one of several supplying what it called "the variety known as Irish". Despite coming from a five-acre site in Edinburgh, the whisky was declared to be "precisely similar to that which is made in Dublin".

Unlike the big urban distillers of Ireland, Scottish blenders had to source their malts from a wider area. Having relied principally on those in Campbeltown, the Lowlands and the Central Highlands, they began to look north. Meanwhile the railways, which had already stretched upwards to Aberdeen and Inverness, began to branch out into Speyside. For all the romantic imagery of smugglers and illicit whisky, it was probably the advent of the Strathspey railway in 1863 that did more to create the biggest epicentre of malt whisky production in Scotland. Distilleries popped up beside the track like homesteads in the American Midwest. Typically they would connect to the main line via a siding and would have their own tank engine, or pug, to transport the sacks of grain and coal in and the newly filled barrels of whisky out.

"The future of the wine trade is whisky," declared the *Wine Trade Review* in 1886, and the orderly spread of distilleries down the Spey valley turned into a stampede. A staggering 33 distilleries were built in Scotland in the last decade of the nineteenth century, two-thirds of them in this one region. There was plentiful East Coast barley nearby, no shortage of water or fuel, an established skilled workforce, easy money from banks and private investors and a seemingly insatiable demand from the blenders. What could possibly go wrong? Step forward one Robert Patterson Pattison and his brother Walter Gilchrist Gray Pattison.

### THE PATTISON CRASH

"The booming of the cannon is nothing to the booming of Pattison's whisky," thundered an advertisement featuring the massed ranks of a Highland artillery regiment. It was typical hubris from the Pattison brothers of Leith, who left the humdrum world of dairy wholesaling to leap into bed with this sexy new spirit. They set up as blenders in 1887 and floated the company on the London Stock Exchange two years later. It was said that the offer was six times oversubscribed.

They soon had a lavish, marbled HQ in Leith and a giant warehouse, and they hired 150 salesmen – more than their much larger rival, DCL. They were also spending an

**TOP LEFT** The late Victorian whisky boom was a battle between the Scots and the Irish, and the smart money was on the Irish. In 1878 the Distillers Co. built the Phoenix Park distillery in Dublin and claimed the country's whisky was five times greater than Scotch.

**ABOVE** A suitably bombastic advert from the Pattison brothers of Leith whose blend became one of the biggest spirits brands in the country before the company crashed in spectacular fashion in 1899, almost bringing the entire whisky industry down with it.

unprecedented £60,000 on advertising by 1898 – around £5 million in today's money. As well as adverts full of imperial bombast, the firm recruited 500 African grey parrots and taught them to squawk in endless repetition, "Buy Pattison's whisky!" – or so it was claimed.

Financed by debt and engaged in some creative accounting, the Pattison brothers, who were by now as rich as Croesus, could only keep it up so long as Scotch whisky itself kept growing. At the start of the 1890s there was just under two million gallons of malt whisky in Scotland's warehouses. By 1898 the amount had soared to over 13 million, and in December the Clydesdale Bank pulled the plug on Pattison's. Its crash brought down nine other companies in its wake and bankrupted scores of small suppliers. Three years later the two brothers were sent down for 9–18 months for fraud and embezzlement. Yet what had happened was a classic speculative bubble that would have burst with or without the Pattisons.

## HANGOVER AND IDENTITY CRISIS

The Scotch whisky industry entered the twentieth century awash with stock and gripped by the worst hangover in its history. The Pattison affair left a deep impression on William Ross, the newly appointed MD of the Distillers Company, who vowed to bring supply and demand closer together and ensure there would be no repetition of the reckless speculation that had caused the crash. Ailing distilleries and blenders were bought up and, if necessary, closed down. Within two decades all the top-selling blends – Johnnie Walker, Dewar's, White Horse and Buchanan's – were under the DCL umbrella.

Meanwhile there was the question of whisky's identity. What exactly was Scotch? Should it be wholly or mainly malt whisky, or did it not matter? Did it even need to come from Scotland? Having stamped out some "adulterated brandy" in 1905,

**OPPOSITE ABOVE:** DCL spent the interwar years buying up its rivals and closing down surplus distilleries to emerge as the big white whale of the whisky trade.

**BELOW** David Lloyd George, Britain's Chancellor of the Exchequer (1908–15) and then wartime Prime Minister, was a thorn in the side of the whisky industry. While he never succeeded in his crusade to "abolish thirst", he did clobber the trade with tax.

Islington Council in London turned on some so-called "Fine Old Scotch". This led to a Royal Commission in 1908 where both sides – the Highland malt mafia and the grain whisky barons like DCL, put their case. Interestingly, had the malt distillers backed a proposal from Alexander Walker for a 50 per cent minimum malt content in blends, the history of Scotch would have been very different. Sir Peter Mackie, the father of White Horse and the whisky baron most closely linked to malt whisky, was able to concede that the blenders may have had the industry's best interests at heart. As he put it later: "Had the trade in whisky been confined to malt, unmellowed by grain spirit, the trade would not be a tenth of what it is today."

In the end the Commission failed to resolve anything. Yet by 1909 a bigger threat loomed in the shape of Lloyd George's budget, which pushed the price of a standard blend to over half a crown (2s.6d.). Many in the industry saw it as a death knell, and part of the Liberal chancellor's crusade to "abolish thirst". Temperance had a long history, with the first temperance society in Scotland founded in 1829, and for a century excise duty had made up 30–40 per cent of government revenue – far more than income tax.

Yet there had never been a moral dimension to excise duty until now. The only good news for the whisky industry was the growth of exports to 7.5 million proof gallons by 1909, Australia being the biggest consumer, followed by the US, Canada and South Africa.

"D·C·L"
PURE SCOTCH WHISKY
FOR EXPORT ONLY

**The Distillers Company, Ltd.,**
EDINBURGH.
Proprietors of
'Highland Club' & 'Caledonian' Whiskies.
AGENTS ALL OVER THE WORLD.

Defenders of the Empire

1924

FROM THE PICTURE PRODUCED BY RAPHAEL TUCK & SONS L?
FOR
MACDONALD, GREENLEES & WILLIAMS ( DISTILLERS ) L?
LEITH LONDON ABERDEEN & GLASGOW
SOLE PROPRIETORS OF
CLAYMORE, OLD PARR AND SANDY MACDONALD
SCOTCH WHISKIES

# THE GREAT WAR AND PROHIBITION

Within a year of the outbreak of the First World War in 1914, Lloyd George was telling the nation there was a more damning threat than German U-boats. "We are fighting Germany, Austria and drink; and as far as I can see the greatest of these deadly foes is drink."

The forces ranged against alcohol had become increasingly politicized. In 1901 the Scottish Prohibition Party was co-founded by Edwin Scrymgeour, who became a Dundee councillor and eventually the city's MP in 1922. After that election, in which he defeated none other than Winston Churchill, he held the seat as the only Prohibitionist MP in Parliament until 1931.

Back in 1914 at the outbreak of the First World War, there was a clamour to ban distilling altogether. The industry, led by the redoubtable William Ross, head of DCL, retaliated by arguing that distilling was essential for the war effort. It provided yeast for baking bread, dope for waterproofing aeroplane wings, and spirit for use in anaesthetics and for making high explosives.

RIGHT New York speakeasy in 1933 in the dying days of Prohibition.

Though malt distilling pretty much ceased, the grain distilleries kept going, allowing Dewar's to supply some three million bottles of its White Label blend to the Army and Navy catering corps. Meanwhile two issues concerning whisky were resolved during the war. By 1917, the minimum strength had been set at 40 per cent alcohol by volume (80 proof) and the spirit had to be aged in oak casks for a minimum of three years before it could be called Scotch whisky.

The price of a bottle of Scotch had been fixed at 12 shillings. After the war this was raised by half a shilling, while the duty was doubled and then raised again, squeezing the big blenders in the process. The resentment of whisky drinkers for having to pay 12s.6d. was given vent in a popular music hall refrain: "How can a fella be happy – when happiness costs such a lot?" And yet at least whisky was still legal on this side of the Atlantic.

## BOOTLEGGERS AND SPEAKEASIES

On the pretext of ensuring that cereals and fruit were kept solely for the food chain, alcohol production was banned in America when the country entered the First World War in 1917. By December of that year the Anti-Saloon League led by the ruthless political lobbyist, Wayne Wheeler, helped to ram a prohibition amendment through Congress. It was eventually passed in January 1919 and became law a year later.

In the months before, drinks like Scotch whisky flooded in, and those with means, including plenty of congressmen, stockpiled whatever they could for the dry years ahead. Within hours of Prohibition there was a foretaste of things to come when an armed gang seized a lorry carrying medicinal alcohol in Chicago.

Surgical spirit was allowed, as was industrial alcohol and the use of alcohol for sacramental purposes. All three became widely exploited loopholes over the next 13 years. What was left of the trade simply disappeared underground as bars became "speakeasies", and legitimate spirits morphed into moonshine or "bathtub gin". By 1925 estimated consumption had fallen by as much as 60 per cent of its pre-Prohibition level, but thereafter it began to rise. It did so because in the public mind the case for Prohibition had never really been won, and because it went against human nature. The American lyricist, Vaughan Miller, put it succinctly:

There ain't going to be no more whiskey
There ain't going to be no more gin
There ain't going to be no more highballs to put
the whiskey in
There ain't going to be no more cigarettes to make folks
pale and thin
But you can't take away that tendency to sin, sin, sin.

BELOW Sam Bronfman, the Canadian liquor baron who made a fortune from bootlegging during Prohibition and went on to found the Seagram empire.

While the Americans may have drunk less, they drank proportionately more spirits, not least because spirits offered the bootleggers better margins than beer or wine. In cities like New York, there was a certain thrill in slipping into an illicit drinking den where many new cocktails were spawned to mask the rough moonshine underneath – by the late 1920s America was the world's biggest importer of cocktail shakers. Eighty years later, a rash of retro "speakeasy" bars began popping up to re-create that mix of glamour and subterfuge of the Prohibition era.

### IN SEARCH OF LIQUOR

Back in Scotland it was soon clear that American demand for whisky had not been choked off. Instead it was flooding over the world's longest international border from Canada, and from what became known as Rum Row. This was the line just beyond US territorial waters where trade could be done between the middlemen and the actual smugglers. Like an auction house with dubious ethics, the trick for Scotch whisky distillers was to keep the "fence" at a distance.

Berry Brothers & Rudd, a pillar of the establishment among London wine merchants, was heavily involved in the trade through Cutty Sark – the blend it created in 1923. That the firm was involved in spirits came to the attention of the notorious gangster Jack Diamond who, with his five quashed convictions for homicide, was not a typical Berry's customer. Known as "Legs" Diamond for his skill on the dance floor, he travelled to Europe in search of liquor.

History is hazy over the precise details of his request for 300 cases of "gen-U-ine" Scotch whisky for cash in the early 1920s. No one really knows whether he came in person to the Berry Bros shop in St James's Street, but it would have been quite a scene.

While blends like Cutty Sark were coming in from Nassau, Sam Bronfman and his clan were extremely busy on the Canadian border. Having set up as the Canada Pure Drug Co. in 1918, they secured the agency for Dewar's and established a string of so-called boozoriums along the Saskatchewan–North Dakota border. As well as legitimate blends like Dewar's, the Bronfmans offered cheaper alternatives like *Parker's Old Irish, Johnny Walker* and that "well-known" malt – *Glen Levitt*. The real cheap stuff was made in an oak-lined tank from distilled water, alcohol, sulphuric acid and a little caramel. The acid would eat into the wood to somehow replicate the ageing process. But unlike some of their rivals, the Bronfmans never used adulterated spirit or the embalming fluid which was sold by a Minneapolis undertaker for a dollar a gallon.

BELOW Britain's only Prohibitionist MP, Edwin Scrymgeour, who beat Winston Churchill in Dundee in the 1922 election and held the seat until 1931.

# CHANGING TIMES

US Prohibition ended on 5 December 1933, having collapsed under the weight of its unintended consequences. It had caused significant unemployment from bottling lines to breweries and liquor stores, had depleted State revenue of drink tax, and had passed an industry worth US$3 billion into the hands of organized crime.

The repeal of Prohibition was great news for the Scotch whisky industry, which had been suffering bleak times at home, where a cash-strapped government had ramped up excise duty. Sales were badly down anyway thanks to the Depression, and by the summer of 1933 there were only two malt distilleries in Scotland still operating– Glenlivet and Glen Grant.

The promised, pent-up demand from America took a while to come through because of initially high tariffs, but by 1939 the US was importing over 4.5 million gallons out of a total production of almost 38 million. By the outbreak of the Second World War the number of distilleries back in operation had climbed to 92, though that soon dwindled as supplies of imported grain grew scarcer. Whisky drinkers at home were hit by higher taxes to help the war effort, though this encouraged a vibrant black market to spring up. Meanwhile the government did what it could to encourage whisky exports, particularly to the States, to help Britain's balance of trade.

### TRANSATLANTIC CONVOYS SET SAIL

Merchant ships would rendezvous in Loch Ewe between Skye and Ullapool, and then set off in convoy across the Atlantic. Among them, in February 1941, was the SS *Politician* which had been loaded with a quarter of a million bottles of Scotch. It ran aground near the tip of South Uist by the island of Eriskay, where the grateful locals helped themselves to precious bottles. The ending by shipwreck of a prolonged whisky drought was the inspiration for Compton Mackenzie's *Whisky Galore!*

Despite treacherous rocks and prowling U-boats, plenty of whisky did get through, although Scotland's distilleries had all shut by 1943 until restrictions on grain were lifted a year later. There were fears that the industry would be crippled beyond repair when the war ended, but it had an ally in the Prime Minister. In April 1945, in a famous memo, Winston Churchill wrote: "On no account reduce the barley for whisky. This takes years to mature and is an invaluable export and dollar producer. Having regard to all our other difficulties about export, it would be improvident not to preserve this characteristic British element of ascendancy." This was not something Lloyd George would have ever written. Churchill's favourite spirit was actually cognac, though most mornings he drank a very weak Johnnie Walker on ice – known within the family as a "Papa Cocktail". He considered the four essentials of life to be "hot baths, cold champagne, new peas and old brandy".

**BELOW LEFT** At 5.32pm, Eastern Standard Time, on 5 December 1933 Utah became the 36th State to ratify the 21st Amendment bringing an end to Prohibition and a near 14-year drought. Yet despite the headline many Americans were already back on the booze by then.

**BELOW** Based on a true story, Compton Mackenzie's famous novel became a box-office hit when the Ealing comedy Whisky Galore was released in 1949.

## SEAGRAM'S LEADS THE WAY

In *The Making of Scotch Whisky*, John Hume and Michael Moss concluded: "By the end of the Second World War, the Scotch whisky industry had endured forty-five years of adversity." Many firms had gone to the wall, or been bought up by the ever-expanding Distillers Company, which had been formed from the merger of the big three blending houses, and later swallowed up its two biggest rivals. Yet the company's big brands, notably Johnnie Walker, Dewar's and White Horse, were run like separate fiefdoms. Meanwhile the North Americans were now major players in the industry, led by Seagram's, who bought Chivas Brothers in 1949 for £85,000 – around £2.7 million today.

Britain's war-torn economy emerged blinking into the 1950s with a desperate need for foreign cash. Scotch whisky was a high-value commodity that could not be made anywhere else and thus fitted the bill perfectly. With rationing at home and a black market that allegedly accounted for one in three bottles drunk, there was every incentive to look abroad. Indeed the post-war Labour government only released barley to the distillers on the basis that at least two-thirds of production was shipped overseas.

**BELOW** Glen Keith was one of the new post-war distilleries built by Seagram to provide malt whisky for its top-selling blends like Chivas Regal and 100 Pipers.

## THE SPIRIT OF THE AMERICAN DREAM

Scotch whisky was dispatched to all corners of the Commonwealth, to the old colonial outposts and far-flung emerging markets from Patagonia to Papua New Guinea. Yet nothing could rival the booming middle-class consumption in the US, particularly during the 1960s. By 1968 American consumers were drinking around 160 million bottles of Scotch a year, up almost three times since the start of the decade. Among the favoured brands were Dewar's White Label, Cutty Sark and J&B Rare, while fighting it out among 12-year-old deluxe blends were Johnnie Walker Black Label and Chivas Regal.

"It was Mr Sam [Bronfman]'s intention to make Chivas Regal the greatest name in Scotch whisky. This was not just a man marketing a new product – it was an artist producing his chef d'oeuvre," a colleague wrote of the Seagram boss. In 1962 Chivas donned its glitzy metallic packaging, and enjoyed a new marketing campaign. It was a smooth blend – "No back bite. No gasp. No wince. No shudder". For US whisky drinkers it was almost the spirit of the American Dream.

## NEW AND ONCE QUIET DISTILLERIES SPRING UP

In 1959 Seagram built Glen Keith, the first new distillery in Scotland since the late Victorian whisky boom; it was the starting gun for a new surge in production which, in the case of grain whisky, had more than doubled by 1966. This was the result of big new grain distilleries at Invergordon and Girvan. Before long malt whisky was catching up.

Everywhere disused distilleries were dragged out of retirement and the stills fired into life, while others like Glenturret and Caperdonich were rebuilt. Many added more stills, including Glenfarclas and Dalmore which were doubled, and five completely new distilleries were built, four from scratch and one – Deanston in Perthshire – converted from an old cotton mill. Of the new distilleries, the most striking was Tormore on Speyside. Constructed in 1960 of pale granite with massive arched windows and a chimney stack shaped like a whisky bottle, it symbolized the industry's post-war confidence like nothing else. Sadly the good times were not to last.

BELOW A scale model of Tormore distillery kept at the Scotch Whisky Heritage Centre in Edinburgh. The Speyside distillery built in 1960 with massive arched windows and a chimney stack shaped like a whisky bottle symbolized the industry's post-war confidence.

# THE WHISKY LOCH AND THE RISE OF MALTS

**The production of Scotch whisky continued to expand throughout the 1970s as though the sales graph would continue its upward trajectory ad infinitum.**

Exports did keep growing until 1978, reaching the equivalent of almost 100 million bottles, but demand in what was by far the biggest market – the USA – had peaked a few years earlier. Many whisky firms had failed to recruit new drinkers, and their brands were fading into retirement like their loyal fans, while that hip, cosmopolitan spirit known as vodka was making waves on both sides of the Atlantic. In America a new generation simply didn't want to drink the same old J&B, Cutty or "Doo-ers" as their old man.

Back in Scotland, alarm bells were ringing on the bridge of the good ship whisky, with over a billion gallons of stock sitting in distillery warehouses by 1975. It was time to hit the brakes, but as with any super-tanker there's a big time lag between doing so and actually slowing down. Unlike vodka, which can be sold as soon as it is cold from the still, every drop of Scotch whisky has to spend at least three years in wood until it can be designated as such.

**BELOW** Port Ellen on Islay, one of nine DCL distilleries that closed for good in 1983, although the Port Ellen Maltings, which supplies the island's distilleries with most of their malt, is still going strong.

To make things harder, there was not just one captain on the bridge but many, given all the industry bosses who each had their own sales forecasts.

In Britain the introduction of VAT in 1982, together with that year's duty increase, added £1.20 to the price of a standard bottle of Scotch. With the whisky loch full to the brim, DCL culled 11 of its 45 distilleries in May 1983, of which only Knockdhu and Benromach were later resuscitated. A year later the company closed another batch of distilleries, including four that never reopened. The fate of a "mothballed" distillery often depended on location. If it was out in the wilds, it might remain dormant for decades before resurrection when Scotch whisky's fortunes were on the rise again, while those in cities were soon sold off and redeveloped. Inverness lost all three of its distilleries at this time, including Glen Albyn whose bones lie buried beneath a shopping mall.

Scotch was losing out in the UK both to white spirits like Smirnoff and Bacardi and to wine, whose sales had trebled in a generation by the 1990s. The tax on wine was slashed by 20 per cent in 1984 to comply with EU rules, while spirits like whisky were hammered by successive chancellors. All this had an impact on the once mighty DCL, but many of its problems were self-inflicted. Having seen its share of the domestic whisky market collapse from 75 per cent in the early 1960s to just 16 per cent, it now found that the predators were at the gates. The Argyll Group, led by James Gulliver, made a hostile bid for the company in 1985. At £1.9 billion it was then the largest offer in UK history, but DCL turned to Guinness to be its saviour. In the end the beer giant triumphed with an offer of £2.7 billion and the combined group became United Distillers & Vintners, or UDV. The deal reeked of scandal, however, and Ernest Saunders, the boss of Guinness, was convicted of fraud and sent to prison. He was released after just 10 months suffering from acute senile dementia, from which he then made a "miraculous" recovery.

## THE GREAT SINGLE MALT REVIVAL

Single malt whisky made in a copper pot still was the original Scotch, before the advent of blends following the invention of the continuous still in the 1820s. So completely did blends take over, that the taste of malt whisky virtually disappeared. It was obviously known to the distillery manager and his friends, and perhaps to some of the locals. Beyond Scotland, a small band of connoisseurs knew where to unearth bottles of Macallan, Talisker and the like, but that was about it.

By 1964 William Grant & Sons was having some success with its Glenfiddich five-year-old malt in Scotland, and decided it deserved a wider audience. It was relaunched as an eight-year-old pure malt in a patented, triangular dark bottle with a grand, silvery label not unlike Chivas Regal. Glenfiddich seeped southwards into England and then abroad, initially via duty-free, and by 1970 annual sales had reached 24,000 cases. The big whisky companies doubted whether single malts would ever catch on with consumers who had been taught, through endless adverts, to appreciate the smooth, mellow nature of blends. Distillers loved to boast how these were greater than the sum of their parts, and how they resembled an orchestra where the malts and the grain whiskies were the instruments. On their own, malts seemed too pungent, raw and full of flavour to ever seduce mainstream whisky drinkers – at least that was the view of many in the industry.

The independents like Macallan and Glenmorangie soon followed Glenfiddich's lead by laying down stock and releasing their own aged malts. Others joined in, yet even by 1980 single malts accounted for less

**BELOW** Glen Grant five-year-old became a huge success in Italy, outselling all other whisky brands, whether blended or single malt. The Speyside distillery is now owned by the Italian spirits giant, Campari.

than 1 per cent of all Scotch whisky. At the time the place where you were most likely to come across them was Italy. The country's regional importers would come over to Scotland and buy casks for bottling under the distillery name. The leading malt was Glen Grant five-year-old, whose sales had passed 200,000 cases by 1977, making it the country's biggest-selling whisky of all.

Finally the big white whale of the industry – UDV (the predecessor to Diageo) – decided in 1988 to release the Classic Malts range, based on the key whisky regions. Representing Islay and Skye were Lagavulin and Talisker, along with Glenkinchie for the Lowlands, Oban for the West Coast, Dalwhinnie for the Highlands and Cragganmore for Speyside. They were picked as picturesque distilleries producing single malt. Judging by the size of Oban, for example, with its solitary pair of stills, no one foresaw how popular the range, and single malts in general, would become. They now account for a tenth of all the Scotch whisky drunk.

**BELOW** Glenfiddich pioneered the modern era of single malt whisky when it launched its eight-year-old in the mid-1960s. Before long it was replaced with a 12-year-old to compete directly with deluxe blends like Chivas Regal and Johnnie Walker Black Label.

PART TWO

ON THE WHISKY TRAIL

# ISLAY

Of all Scotland's whisky regions, Islay has by far the strongest identity. Being an island obviously plays a big part, but there is also its famous signature tune of peat smoke embraced by all of Islay's distilleries with the exception of Bunnahabhain. There was never a conscious decision to produce peaty whiskies; it was simply that peat was the only source of fuel available on the island. People heated their crofts with a central fire from which the pungent, blue smoke wafted its way towards a hole in the roof. Since none of the internal walls reached up to the ceiling, people's clothes, bedding and hair would have been as smoky as an old kipper. As such, the idea of an unpeated whisky would have been unthinkable. It just wouldn't have been whisky.

# THE WHISKY HERITAGE OF ISLAY

Of all Scotland's whisky regions, Islay has by far the strongest identity. Being an island obviously plays a big part, but there is also its famous signature tune of peat smoke embraced by all of Islay's distilleries, apart from Bunnahabhain. There was never a conscious decision to produce peaty whiskies; it was simply that peat was the only fuel source on the island.

People heated their crofts with a fire in the middle from which the pungent, blue smoke wafted its way towards a hole in the roof. Since none of the internal walls reached up to the ceiling, people's clothes, bedding and hair would have been as smoky as an old kipper. As such, the idea of an unpeated whisky would have unthinkable. It just wouldn't have been whisky.

On Islay there has never been a shortage of water for distilling. Although the island's highest hills are barely 1,500 feet, they still scrape the bottom of passing rain clouds rolling in off the Atlantic to keep the burns, rivers and bogs topped up. Of course Islay shares this damp climate with the rest of the Western Isles, but more unique was its access to barley. Arable farming on Islay may be almost unsustainable nowadays, but it is the most fertile of the Hebrides. It grew enough cereal for the island's early distillers before the first imported grain arrived in 1815. Their whisky may have contained oats and wheat and was no doubt sweetened with bog myrtle, thyme and wild mint.

The amount of whisky distilled on the island's farms depended on the harvest. In good years there was no conflict with the grain needed for food, but in poor years it could result in famine. Over on the mainland the authorities were extending their control over whisky and viewing it as an important source of tax revenue after the Act of Union of 1707. But when the Glasgow MP Daniel Campbell voted for the unpopular Malt Tax in 1725, the mob burnt his house down. With the compensation he was paid, he bought Islay for £6,000 and with his descendants, helped modernize farming on the island.

The first exciseman, or *gauger,* arrived here in the 1790s and discovered a vibrant cottage industry of illicit distillation and smuggling.

## 1,500-YEAR SECRET

With the coast of Ireland less than 30 miles away, the secret of distillation may have arrived with Catholicism in those coracles rowed by sixth-century Irish monks. It is known that whisky-making was established well before the island's first licensed distillery of Bowmore was founded in 1779. Word of the island's whisky reached the Royal Household, who twice requested "a cask of your best Islay Mountain Dew" from the Campbell's in the 1840s. The demand for these malt whiskies continued into the early twentieth century, though by then, most of the production was disappearing into blends.

Blenders clearly rated Islay malts and were willing to pay a premium price, but they viewed them as a "top dressing" to be used sparingly. If the malt were particularly pungent a teaspoon might suffice, whereas the same blend might contain a third or more of Speyside malt.

The fate of any malt distillery was tied to the fortunes of blended Scotch. When the industry was full of confidence, production would be cranked up, but whenever there was a surfeit of Scotch, the stills would be turned down or even stopped. On Islay this issue was compounded by the steady contraction within the industry. If a whisky giant gobbled up a rival and found it now owned two distilleries there, it would often close one of them. Yet the island's remoteness helped mothballed distilleries survive, as there was less risk of being bulldozed into history during a downturn as sometimes happened on the mainland. However, what really turned Islay's fortunes around was the boom in single malts.

Each of the island's seven historic distilleries, plus boutique newcomers like Kilchoman and now Ardnahoe, enjoy a strong identity through their single malts. Names like Lagavulin, Bruichladdich and Ardbeg, once barely known outside the industry, are now world famous, and draw ever more whisky pilgrims to the island.

# ARDBEG

Ardbeg is the furthest flung of the three distilleries in the Kidalton area on Islay's south-east coast, the others being Laphroaig and Lagavulin. With the Kintyre peninsula on the mainland just 15 miles by boat, the area had long been a hot-bed of whisky smuggling, as a Kildalton parish report from the 1770s makes clear: "We have not an excise officer in the whole island. The quantity therefore of whisky made here is very great; and the evil that follows drinking to excess of this liquor, is very visible on this island."

In 1798 the McDougalls – a family of tenant farmers, took out a lease to farm here, and John McDougall was probably distilling whisky before Ardbeg was officially founded in 1815. His son Alexander became a well-known figure in the Glasgow spirits trade and built Ardbeg's reputation there. He was fiercely proud of his name and once paid the fine of a fellow clansman in court on the grounds it was impossible for a McDougall to do wrong.

By the time of his death in 1853, Ardbeg was supporting a 200-strong community which soon had its own school. Ownership of the distillery passed to Alexander's sisters, Margaret and Flora, who were entered in a lease at the time as "co-partners" carrying on business at Ardbeg as distillers under the firm of Alexander MacDougall & Co. Whether they really were "Scotland's first lady distillers" is hard to know, for the old laird's former coachman was also down as managing the distillery. This was Colin Hay, who became owner of Ardbeg on the demise of the sisters, and continued to send the whisky to Buchanan's – a firm of whisky merchants in Glasgow who later became partners in the distillery.

### FROM LONELY TO ALLIED

When the Victorian whisky writer Alfred Barnard visited in the 1880s he spoke of the distillery's lonely position on the very verge of the sea and how "the isolation tends to heighten the romantic sense of its position". From its pair of spirit stills it was then producing 250,000 gallons of Pure Islay Malt a year, which Buchanan's sold on to the big wine and spirit merchants in Glasgow, Liverpool and London. In the space of 50 years it had grown from a small farmyard operation pumping out just 500 gallons a week into a relatively big, full-fledged distillery with a staff of 60.

The firm of Alexander MacDougall & Co. carried on until the 1950s, the distillery having been bought outright from the laird of Kildalton in the 1920s for £19,000. In 1973 Ardbeg was swallowed up by the Canadian giant Hiram Walker and the Distillers Company, with the former gaining full control four years later. In turn Hiram Walker became part of Allied Distillers, who also owned its near neighbour, Laphroaig.

Allied's MD, the late Alistair Cunningham, reportedly described Ardbeg as "heaven's own nectar", and said that "if you knew exactly the amount to take each day you could live for ever". Despite that, Ardbeg was essentially a blending ingredient, and its main role was to give the smooth, bestselling Ballantine's brand a slight smoky edge. Only Laphroaig was pushed as a single malt, and when the Scotch industry entered a prolonged slump in the 1980s, its owners decided they could live without two Islay distilleries. Ardbeg ceased production in 1982, then reopened in 1989 only to close again in 1996, possibly for ever. Empty and forlorn with

LEFT Given the almost cult-like status of Ardbeg among fans of peat-soaked Islay malts, it is hard to believe that the distillery almost vanished in the 1980s at the height of the whisky loch was at its peak.

its pagoda roof encased in scaffolding, it looked as if Ardbeg had reached the end of the road.

In 1997 it was bought for £7.1 million by the Glenmorangie company, who had to spend a few more million on repairs. The new owners acquired the aged stock, but there were serious holes in the inventory. In 2004 they were able to release a six-year-old "Very Young" Ardbeg, followed by "Still Young" and "Almost There", until finally they were able to launch a regular, 10-year-old flagship malt. Given the trend towards removing age-statements altogether from single malts, you wonder if Ardbeg's owners would have been so concerned today.

## MORE SMOKE WITH NO FAN

The gaps in Ardbeg's warehouse have led to some creative blending between vintages and a profusion of different, limited-release expressions with varying degrees of peaty-ness. Along the way there has been Ardbeg Blasda – a third as smoky as the standard 10-year-old, and the intensely phenolic Ardbeg Supernova. Meanwhile cask strength expressions have included Uigedal, named after one of the lochs that supply Ardbeg's water, and "Alligator", matured in heavily re-charred Bourbon barrels. It has all helped to build the brand's cult status among its devotees, as has the Ardbeg Committee. This fan club was founded in

**BELOW** "The isolation tends to heighten the romantic sense of its position," wrote Alfred Barnard on his visit to Ardbeg in the 1880s.

2000 and meets by the ancient Kildalton Cross at midnight, or so it is said.

Ardbeg has a reputation for being one of the smokiest whiskies of all with its flavours of soot and tar, though there are a number of lighter expressions that challenge that. Its original distillers certainly knew of the importance of local peat, which was used to fuel the kiln and malt the barley until the 1960s. This was typical practice, but what set Ardbeg apart was the absence of fans in the pagoda roof to draw the smoke through the barley. As a result the grain was drenched in peat smoke for that much longer. Today the malt comes from the nearby Port Ellen maltings and, interestingly, the level of peat smoke is more or less the same as for Laphroaig and Lagavulin.

What sets all three apart is the way they are distilled, the shape of the stills and the differences in maturation. One reason why Ardbeg can cope with such highly peated malt is the curious piece of copper tubing attached to the wash still which helps purify the wash before sending it through to the spirit still. It is claimed that if you put Ardbeg's wash through a standard spirit still, the result would be undrinkable. The increased contact with the copper gives a faint sweetness to the spirit to balance the smoke.

# WHISKY TASTING NOTES
## ARDBEG UIGEADAIL 54.2% ABV

Pronounced "Oog-a-dal" and named after the loch that supplies Ardbeg's water, Uigeadail is a vatting of the traditional 10-year-old with older malts that have been matured in sherry casks. The combination of the resinous, citrus peel notes from the sherry with the typical peat-soaked flavours of Ardbeg 10 is nothing if not intense, especially if sipped neat at cask strength. Yet even without water this earthy, mouth-filling dram is surprisingly smooth. It has a leathery texture and notes of spice, black treacle, liquorice and tar, but manages to maintain a fine balance of smoke and sweetness on the tongue. With a little water the smoke seems to intensify. In a word, it's a big whisky, and not for the faint-hearted.

# BOWMORE ISLE OF ISLAY, ARGYLL AND BUTE

For the residents of Bowmore, the island's capital, the local distillery is the first line of defence against the Atlantic storms that occasionally blow in through the open jaws of Loch Indaal. Its warehouses are literally built into the harbour wall, and are often bathed in sea spray if not battered by the waves themselves. "The distillery's proximity to the sea plays a vital role in shaping the final character of our spirit, which breathes in the salty sea air all the while it's maturing," declares the Bowmore website.

**BELOW** Distilled right on the edge of Loch Indaal, Bowmore is a true maritime malt whose casks soak in the salty sea spray from the air, or so it is claimed.

Sniff deeply and take a sip, and there is something brisk and saline in this maritime malt, though no chemical analysis has ever revealed any trace of salt in the whisky. Most of Islay's distillers age their malts on the mainland and would tell you that where they are matured is of little consequence to the finished product. To which Bowmore might respond: "Well, they would say that, wouldn't they?" Bowmore sits on some 27,000 casks in its three warehouses.

What is beyond question is that Bowmore is the oldest surviving distillery on Islay; indeed it is one of the oldest in Scotland. It was founded in 1779, barely a decade after this pretty whitewashed village was established by

Daniel Campbell, the laird of Islay whose grandfather bought the island in 1726. The distillery quickly became a focal point for the community, along with the church, which is famously round. It was built that way, allegedly, to deny the devil any corner where he might hide and lure any unwitting member of the congregation into sin.

The Bowmore distillery was founded at the bottom of Hill Street down by the water-front by a local entrepreneur, John Simpson. He came from a nearby village at the foot of Loch Indaal, and had been granted rights to open a quarry and build houses here as well as cut turf from the moss. He was also the local postmaster, ran a steam packet from Port Askaig to Tarbert on the mainland, and there is even some evidence that he did some distilling on Jura as well.

## BROTHERS MAKE BOWMORE GROW

How important the distillery was among Simpson's various business ventures is unclear, and Bowmore probably remained very small scale until it was acquired by twin brothers William and James Mutter in 1837. These Glasgow merchants of German extraction were determined to drag the distillery into the industrial age and expand the market for its whisky. James Mutter happened to be the Glaswegian vice-consul for the Ottoman Empire, Portugal and Brazil.

The still-house was expanded and new kilns and warehouses were added, while the number of stills had grown to four by the 1880s. According to a contemporary etching these were all different and included a weird double-headed still that fed into two separate worm tubs – a radical design that never caught on. Because of the expansion, the water supply that came from the River Laggan had to be diverted into a nine-mile aqueduct to carry sufficient water to feed the mash. At the time production of this "pure Islay malt" had risen to 200,000 gallons a year, making Bowmore second only to Ardbeg in scale. The Mutters had their own 145-ton steamship to carry the casks to the mainland, where it was aged and bottled under the arches of Glasgow's Central Station.

Some of it was exported as far afield as Canada.

But something went wrong, and by 1890 the Mutter family had gone out of business. Over the next 70 years a number of new owners came and went, but the distillery kept going, except during the Second World War when it was requisitioned by Coastal Command. After this brief interlude as a base for flying boats on U-boat patrol in the Atlantic, Bowmore was back making whisky. In 1963 it was bought by the Glasgow-based whisky brokers Stanley P. Morrison Ltd, who began to crank up production. Within five years the distillery was pumping out 880,000 gallons per annum – 14 times what it had produced the year before the sale. The firm, which became known as Morrison Bowmore, soon realized what an asset it had. Its business had been all about selling bulk whisky to blenders; now it began to focus on single malts.

## FLOOR MALTINGS

Bowmore took the bold decision to hang on to its own floor maltings at a time when most distilleries were abandoning theirs as an expensive anachronism. Today they only provide a third of the malt needed, but they give Bowmore a real traditional feel. Having been steeped in water, the barley is spread evenly over the stone malting floors, of which there are three. As the

RIGHT A traditional dunnage warehouse beside Bowmore – one of three used to age around 27,000 casks of its whisky. How maturation on the island effects the final flavour is hard to quantify.

grain starts to warm up and begin germinating, it has to be turned every four hours to prevent it matting together. Then, after about a week, it is transported to a wire mesh above the malt kiln to be dried. The dense blue peat smoke weaves its way through the malt and out through the slats in the pagoda roof.

Floor maltings give the distillery a self-sufficient feel, though whether they have any material impact on the final whisky would be difficult to prove. Their main role is really about enhancing the visitor experience, which they undoubtedly do. Somehow the next distillery, with its pagoda roof just there for decoration and completely free of smoke, will never be quite as evocative. And with this in mind, Bowmore were one of the first distilleries to install a visitor's centre.

Those on a distillery tour will hear about warehouse number one, partly below sea level and the oldest in Scotland. They will also hear of the curious fate of warehouse number three which is now the local swimming pool and heated by the waste heat from the still-room next door. Then comes a chance to taste and possibly buy some of the malts. The range was revamped in 2007 and includes "Legend", "Darkest" and a whole raft of aged expressions up to 40-year-old and beyond.

## WHISKY TASTING NOTES
### BOWMORE 12-YEAR-OLD 40% ABV

Like Macallan, this famous distillery – the oldest on Islay – has gone the route of non-age-statement whiskies like Bowmore "Legend" and "Small Batch", but the 12-year-old remains the real flagship whisky and a popular choice for those who want to explore a more subtle side of the island. True to its Islay roots, there is an immediate waft of peat from the glass, but there is a softer, herbal element to the smoke. It is less astringent and medicinal than Islay malts like Laphroaig or Ardbeg. When tasted with a little water, it won't put hairs on your chest like some Islay peat monsters, but you can enjoy this moderately smoky whisky with a beguiling citrus freshness and a light, silky texture.

# BRUICHLADDICH ISLE OF ISLAY, ARGYLL AND BUTE

For years Bruichladdich has revelled in a spirit of defiance that offers a counterblast to all that is corporate and bland in the world of Scotch whisky. Since 2000, when the distillery was bought by an independent consortium, it has been the industry's answer to those self-styled bad boys of British brewing, Scotland's Brewdog. Bruichladdich's independence lasted until 2012 when it was bought by the French spirits group Remy Cointreau for £58 million, though it seems the old ethos remains intact. On its website Bruichladdich still describes itself as a "progressive Hebridean distiller" and proclaims: "We are proudly non-conformist as has always been the way."

Founded in 1881, Bruichladdich was a purpose-built distillery from the start. Instead of evolving out of the farm like so many others, it was a state-of-the-art whisky-making machine with modern cavity walls and concrete – a radical new building material at the time. The concrete was reinforced with pebbles from the sea shore. Built on a hill around a spacious courtyard, it was designed by Robert Harvey, a young engineer from Glasgow. He and his two elder brothers were part of the Glasgow-based whisky dynasty that owned Yoker and Dundas Hill – the largest malt distillery in Scotland at the time.

In the 1880s blended Scotch was really starting to take off, and the blenders were eager to source less dominant malts for the bulk of their blends. Rather than copy the traditional, heavily peated style of the likes of Lagavulin and Ardbeg, Bruichladdich strove to offer the blenders a less smoky, more approachable malt. The style of whisky was probably similar to Bunnahabhain, which was founded on Islay the same year. Soon Bruichladdich's two stills were pumping out 94,000 gallons of malt whisky a year. Every week the grain was shipped in and the barrels were shipped out in small, flat-bottomed steam puffers. Most was bought by the Distillers Company on the understanding that Bruichladdich did not try and bottle any single malt itself.

## BRUICHLADDICH RUNS OUT OF STEAM

The distillery limped along, barely making a profit, until it closed in 1907 and remained so throughout the First World War. In 1919 Robert's nephew, Rudd Harvey, was out in Chile when he received a telegram from his father: "Come home 1st steamer, distillery working." In truth it was still idle and there were two-foot weeds growing in the courtyard as Rudd discovered on his return. But the older generation of Harveys, who had by then lost their distilleries on the mainland, were keen to fire up the stills once more.

This they did until 1929, when Bruichladdich became a casualty of the Depression. A buyer was eventually found in Joseph Hobbs, a Scottish-born entrepreneur who had made and lost a fortune in the States. Hobbs paid just £8,000 in 1936 and then swiftly resold the distillery to another firm he had interests in for three times the amount. Then, having built up reasonable stocks, the distillery was sold again to the Glasgow whisky brokers Ross & Coulter for £205,000 in 1952.

By the late 1950s, with its old steam engine and the barley still hoisted up to the barley loft by horse, Bruichladdich was now far from state-of-the-art. More mergers and acquisitions followed, and the distillery's

**BELOW** Bruichladdich's master distiller, Jim McEwan with a cask sample from the distillery's warehouse. McEwan, who was born on the island and previously worked for Bowmore, has been a lifelong ambassador for Islay malts.

production capacity was doubled to 800,000 gallons with a second pair of stills. But in 1993 its then owners, the Glasgow-based blenders Whyte & Mackay, declared it was "surplus to requirement," and closed it down again. Technically the distillery had been "mothballed", with its equipment looked after as it waited for the cyclical upturn in Scotch whisky's fortunes, but as the years went by hopes of Bruichladdich's resurrection began to fade.

## NEW OWNERS, NEW EXPRESSIONS

The distillery was rescued by a private consortium, led by the wine merchant and independent whisky bottler Mark Reynier, in December 2000. For £6.5 million they acquired a patchy collection of maturing stock and a distillery in desperate need of repair. The winter months were spent patching up the building and distilling equipment until the stills were fired up and the first new spirit flowed at the end of May 2001. At the party to celebrate the event, one very old Ileach, or native of Islay, was heard to say: "This is better than the Coronation."

Having poached Jim McEwan, veteran distiller and Ileach, from Bowmore, the new owners decided to distil, alongside the lighter Bruichladdich, a heavily peated spirit which they called Port Charlotte after a defunct

**BELOW** The picturesque village of Port Charlotte on the shores of Loch Indaal, whose name has been adopted by nearby Bruichladdich for a separate range of malts.

distillery nearby. In the meantime they began to unleash a dizzying array of new expressions and limited releases to exploit what stocks they had in the warehouse. News of every new bottling, however small, was trumpeted to every blogger and whisky writer on the planet to help this remote, one-off distillery to punch above its weight.

Bruichladdich's owners were keen to make the whisky as much part of the island as possible. Initially it was bottled off the island, using Islay water that was sent over to reduce the whisky to bottling strength. In 2003 a bottling line was installed at the distillery and a year later this was followed by "Ugly Betty", Scotland's last surviving Lomond still. It was brought over from the mainland and is now used to make "The Botanist" gin. Jim McEwan and his team even produced an organic single malt made from locally grown "bere" barley.

Other bottlings included a pink whisky, X4 – a high-strength malt distilled four times – and Octomore, which was claimed to be "the most heavily peated whisky in the world". Finally in 2011, Mark Reynier was able to celebrate a decade of continual production at Bruichladdich by launching his first 10-year-old – The Laddie Ten. A year later he stepped down, leaving many of the old team including McEwan with the new French owners.

## WHISKY TASTING NOTES
### BRUICHLADDICH PORT CHARLOTTE SCOTTISH BARLEY 50% ABV

Port Charlotte is the pretty village on the shore of Loch Indaal, two miles south of Bruichladdich, that was home to the Lochindaal distillery for a hundred years until 1929. By all accounts its whisky was drenched in peat, and this expression is Bruichladdich's tribute to it. Pale gold in colour, it certainly has a powerful peat reek, but with less of that iodine and medicinal character you find in the likes of Laphroaig. There is also a distinct burnt caramel sweetness on the nose and some may even detect a slight fruitiness. On the tongue there is a dusty, smoky herbal core which really dominates until other elements emerge including candied fruit and liquorice.

# LAPHROAIG PORT ELLEN, ISLE OF ISLAY, ARGYLL AND BUTE

As a single malt Laphroaig is famed for its ferociously pungent flavour – a mix of tar, sea salt, iodine and smoke, but if you visit the actual distillery you may be slightly disappointed. Lying in its sheltered bay with the low hills of Kildalton behind and a gently shelving sea shore in front, it is certainly pretty. But it doesn't quite live up to the whisky's uncompromising reputation – a single malt that you will either "love or hate", as an old advertising campaign once claimed. Of course if your trip to Laphroaig were to coincide with a full-scale Atlantic storm that would be different. With breakers battering the whitewashed walls of the distillery, it would feel like the perfect place to drink Laphroaig, raw and undiluted.

The name comes from the Gaelic *Lag Bhròdhas*, which roughly translates as "hollow of the broad bay". It was here in the early nineteenth century that Donald and Alexander Johnston leased a thousand acres from the laird of Islay to farm cattle. Soon after, by around 1815, they were making whisky as well. It was a well-chosen spot with a good, consistent supply of water and peat, and Port Ellen just a few miles west. This was the main port on Islay's south coast, where barley could be brought in from the mainland and casks of whisky shipped out. Laphroaig was soon joined by the Ardenistiel distillery next door, which for a while belonged to James and Andrew Stein from the famous dynasty of Lowland distillers. By the 1860s it had been amalgamated into Laphroaig.

Long before then, Alexander Johnston sold his share of the business to his brother for £350 and emigrated to Australia. Donald struggled on alone until his death in 1847. According to some he drowned in a vat of his own bunt ale. The distillery was left in trust to his son Dugald, who was only 11 at the time. Ten years later he took over the running of Laphroaig with his first cousin. As the century progressed the pair started to complain about the raw deal they were getting from their agents – JL Mackie & Co., a firm of whisky merchants in Glasgow who also distributed and later owned Laphroaig's great rival, Lagavulin.

## FOUL PLAY

This rivalry began to turn sour in 1887, when the Johnstons, who were making a loss at the time, decided to terminate the relationship with Mackie's. By that stage Peter Mackie, who was to become one of the great late Victorian whisky barons with the White Horse blend, was working for his uncle's firm. He was deeply attached to Islay whisky and somewhat obsessed with Laphroaig. He fell out with the Johnstons over water rights and ended up in court, having ordered one of his men to choke off Laphroaig's water supply using stones in 1907. The following year Mackie decided to build a replica of the distillery within the ground of Lagavulin which he christened the Malt Mill. Yet despite replicating the stills as carefully as he could, and employing Laphroaig's former head brewer, he never managed to copy the whisky.

When Laphroaig's lease came up for renewal in 1921, Mackie made one final, failed bid to buy the distillery. Instead it remained in the family with a direct descendant, Ian Hunter, who set about expanding capacity with two new spirit stills, a new wash still and a new maltings. With the US officially teetotal since the advent of Prohibition in 1919, Hunter was one of the first

FAR LEFT As one of a handful distilleries to retain its floor maltings, Laphroaig's kiln infuses the grain with dense, blue, peat smoke, although most of its malt comes ready peated from Port Ellen.

LEFT Sir Peter Mackie — or "Restless Peter" as he was known, was the whisky baron with the greatest attachment to malt whisky, particularly from Islay. He owned neighbouring Lagavulin and built a copy of Laphroaig in its grounds, though he never managed to replicate the whisky.

in the Scotch whisky industry to bring in old Bourbon barrels for ageing his spirit. At the time most other distillers in Scotland were using old sherry butts from Spain. The coconut and vanilla flavours of American oak have helped soften the bitter, peat-soaked character of Laphroaig's new-make spirit ever since.

## THE LADY LOVES LAPHROAIG

In the early 1930s Bessie Williamson, who had just graduated from Glasgow University, took a summer job at Laphroaig to help out with admin. She arrived with a single suitcase, but ended up staying for 40 years. With her boss suffering a stroke in 1938 and confined to a wheelchair, she took over as distillery manager – a unique position in an industry dominated by men.

Production was paused during the Second World War, but afterwards the stills were fired up and in 1954 Williamson inherited Laphroaig on the death of Ian Hunter, who had no next of kin. She continued to sell the whisky to blenders and as a single malt, particularly the US, where a certain amount of Laphroaig had been sold legally as a medicinal spirit during Prohibition. In an early BBC interview she explained that "the secret of Islay whiskies is the peaty water and the peat". She also spoke of an increasing demand among whisky drinkers for the island's malts which Laphroaig was struggling to supply.

**BELOW** Laphroaig – "the finest whisky in the world", or so Prince Charles is said to have claimed.

During the 1960s Williamson gradually sold the business to Long John Distillers which was part of the American group Shenley Industries, but continued as distillery manager until her retirement in 1972. Three years later Long John was bought by the brewer Whitbread, who later sold their whisky business to Allied Domecq. Laphroaig then passed back into American ownership in 2005, when it was bought by the owners of Jim Beam, and now belongs to the Japanese as part of Beam-Suntory. Today its Scotch whisky stable-mates include the Teacher's blend and fellow Islay malt Bowmore.

Despite all the changes in ownership, Laphroaig appears in rude health with its Royal coat of arms received from Prince Charles proudly displayed on the label for over two decades. The Prince came in person to do the honours in 1994 and by the time he got to the distillery he may well have needed a drink, having crash-landed the Royal plane on the island's tiny runway. "I hope you continue to use the traditional methods," he apparently told Ian Henderson, the then distillery manager. "I think you make the finest whisky in the world." Among the traditional methods is the continued use of floor maltings which account for a quarter of Laphroaig's needs.

## WHISKY TASTING NOTES
### LAPHROAIG QUARTER CASK 48% ABV

Some years ago Laphroaig decided to revive an old tradition in its warehouses on Islay. Having aged in traditional ex-bourbon barrels used for the distillery's flagship 10-year-old single malt, some is filled into casks a quarter of the normal size which increases the ratio of wood to whisky by a third and therefore speeds up the whole maturation process. However, the effect does not seem to diminish Laphroaig's burst of tarry peat and iodine that the distillery is well known for. Maybe there is an extra layer of vanilla sweetness on the nose, and this becomes more apparent on the tongue, giving a slightly richer texture to the whisky before some dry wood tannins poke through on its lingering finish.

# LAGAVULIN

Lagavulin sits in the middle of the so-called "Kildalton Three" with Ardbeg a mile to the east, and Laphroaig round the next bay to the west. For a while such close proximity bred contempt, or at least fierce rivalry between Lagavulin and Laphroaig, but that has long mellowed into mutual respect. Each produces fine single malts with a hefty bittersweet tang of peat, yet despite being next-door neighbours their whiskies are decidedly different.

Across Lagavulin Bay are the ruins of Dunyvaig Castle, which was once a stronghold of the Lord of the Isles. They kept a fleet of flat-bottomed boats, good for slipping in and out past a vicious set of rocks that lurk just beneath the surface at high tide and guard the entrance to the bay. Adding to the sense of history is the fact that Robert the Bruce is said to have fled here after his defeat by the Earl of Pembroke in the fourteenth century. As for whisky making, that too goes back a long way.

The whisky writer Dave Broom has speculated that this corner of Islay may have been the crucible of distilling in Scotland. When Áine Ó Catháin married Angus MacDonald, Lord of the Isles, in 1300 her wedding party concluded at Dunyvaig Castle. She brought with her the MacBeatha family who became the hereditary physicians to the MacDonalds and who did know the secret of *UisgeBeatha*, the water of life.

Whether some evidence will ever come to light remains to be seen, but what is clear is that by the mid-eighteenth century this strip of coastline was a seething hot-bed of illicit distillation. It appears there was a kind of whisky-making co-operative, with "ten small and separate smuggling bothys for the manufacture of moonlight", to quote Alfred Barnard on his distilleries tour of 1887. Each had its own primitive still, and they were all clustered round a mill that supplied the malted barley.

## MILLS IN A HOLLOW

Out of this emerged Lagavulin whose name comes from the Gaelic *lagganmhouillin* or mill in the hollow. The distillery was founded in 1816 by John Johnston, father of Donald Johnston of Laphroaig. A year later another small distillery founded by the laird, Archibald Campbell, cropped up alongside, and appears to have traded under the name Ardmore during its brief life. It was merged into Lagavulin when Johnston died in 1836 owing money to Alexander Graham, a Glasgow merchant who was married to a local girl.

Graham ran the Islay Cellar with his partner James Logan Mackie, and acquired Lagavulin and a lease on the land for the princely sum of £1,103 9s.8d. The pair were also sole agents for Laphroaig and sold both whiskies as pure Islay malt in and around the Glasgow area. When James Mackie's nephew Peter joined the business in 1878 he was packed off to Lagavulin to study the art of distillation. By all accounts he fell in love with the island and its heavily peated malts.

On his return, Peter Mackie wasted no time in promoting Lagavulin and Laphroaig to a wider audience, while developing trade sales to blenders. By 1884 demand was such that he was able to open an office in London. Back on Islay, Lagavulin was expanded into one of the biggest distilleries on the island with three malt houses and two kilns and an annual production of 75,000 gallons. According to Alfred Barnard, the whisky was floated out in barrels across the bay to ships waiting beyond the rocks.

## BACKING A WINNER

In 1890 Mackie trademarked the name of the blend that was to make

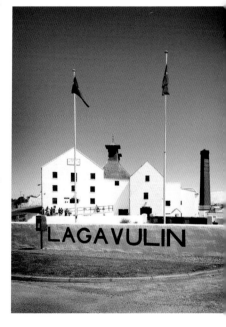

BELOW Officially founded in 1816, Laphroaig's roots may be considerable older. Some claim it was once part of a collection of small smuggling botheys dedicated to 'the manufacture of moonshine'

his fortune. At first White Horse was sold only abroad, but once exports had reached 24,000 cases a year, it was decided to launch the brand in the UK in 1901. By the outbreak of the First World War annual domestic sales were running at 70,000 cases. There was grain whisky and Speyside malt in the blend, but there was always a decent dollop of Lagavulin, which became the spiritual home of White Horse.

Known as "Restless Peter" to his staff, Sir Peter Mackie was the quintessential Scotsman on the make. Having squabbled with his neighbours he tried to make a "Laphroaig-style" whisky from 1908 at the Malt Mill distillery which sat within the grounds of Laphroaig. It was about a fifth the size in terms of production, and reputedly used heather in the mash, along with heavily peated malt. According to Dr Nick Morgan of Lagavulin's parent company Diageo: "As far as anyone knows it was nothing like Laphraoig, albeit it was a pretty good whisky for blending, so they carried on making it for over 50 years."

**BELOW** For its flagship single malt, the casks of Lagavulin slumber for sixteen long years.

One rare blend from the 1930s and 1940s that did contain Malt Mill was Mackie's Ancient Scotch, which gives the distillery as its address. If you have a bottle of it lurking in the back of your drinks cupboard, it could be worth a few thousand pounds. But if you produced some Malt Mill itself, nobody would believe you. It appears it was never bottled as a single malt. At Lagavulin there is one bottle of Malt Mill's new make spirit, sealed with a lump of wax and with a label scribbled in biro. It is believed to be unique, but it's not Scotch whisky, having spent no time in wood.

The Malt Mill closed in 1962 and its two stills were absorbed into Lagavulin. Around that time, the old floor maltings were closed in favour of the Port Ellen maltings nearby. Port Ellen produced its own single malt until it was closed as a distillery in 1983. Five years later, Lagavulin 16-year-old was selected as one of the original six "Classic Malts", whose success guaranteed the distillery's survival. Lagavulin did not completely escape the slow-down in Scotch whisky in the 1980s, and the distillery was put on a three-day week, causing serious supply issues down the line. Thanks to the popularity of its malts, which now include a 12-year-old and a Distiller's Edition, production has long been running at full steam.

# WHISKY TASTING NOTES
## LAGAVULIN 16-YEAR-OLD 43% ABV

Diageo's accountants may rue the day it was decided to fill Lagavulin as a 16-year-old single malt and present it as one of the founder members of the six Classic Malts. But the angels up above must be happy to get their 2% share through evaporation every year, and so too are the whisky's many fans. The prolonged maturation helps tame the medicinal, peat-soaked aromas and give them an extra dimension. Beneath the smoke something more exotic and subtle starts to emerge – a mix of beach bonfires, Lapsang Souchong tea and candied peel. It is a magnificent brute that rolls over the tongue, at first oily and luscious but turning drier and almost mineral with a salty maritime finish.

# WESTERN ISLES

It is one of the great, unsolved mysteries of Scotch whisky that Islay is awash with malt distilleries yet the rest of the Western Isles have so few. In its entire history this necklace of islands, excluding Islay, was home to just 13 licensed distilleries. Seven of them were on the Isle of Skye, which now only has Talisker, while the Isle of Mull has just Tobermory, which spent much of the twentieth century in mothballs and only survived by the skin of its teeth. Yet both are now operating at full steam, and sales of Talisker are said to be booming. In recent years they have been joined by a number of small distilleries, starting with Arran in 1995, followed by Abhainn Dearg on Lewis and, latest of all, the Isle of Harris distillery which went into production in 2015.

# THE WHISKY HERITAGE OF THE WESTERN ISLES

With the exception of Islay and Tiree, the Western Isles have neither the soil nor climate to encourage crop growing, though maybe it was watching some wet grain ferment that first inspired the islanders. Such natural fermentation would have produced a rough beer that could only benefit from distillation.

There were plenty willing to try, as John Knox wrote of Mull on his Hebridean Tour of the 1780s: "Of every year's production of Barley, a third or fourth part is distilled into a spirit called whisky, of which the natives are immoderately fond." Whisky drinking was enshrined in island culture through clan gatherings that invariably featured plenty of *usquebaugh*, or whisky, passed round in a shell, or *Quaich*. The festivities would last for days until the clan elders passed out and had to be carried off in a barrow, or so it was claimed.

In 1609, James IV attempted to curb such competitive feasting with the Statutes of Iona; one of which dealt specifically with the "extraordinary drinking of strong wines and acquavitie." The elders and clan chief were allowed to import a limited quantity of booze from the mainland, though the limits were generous. MacLean of Duart on Mull was allowed up to four tuns of wine a year, equivalent to 18 bottles a day. Common people were denied such imports, though they were allowed to make their own beer and whisky for personal consumption.

In his *Description of the Western Isles* of 1702, Martin Martin was impressed by the amount of whisky drinking and its strength, as shown in the following passage about the Isle of Lewis: "... [the] natives brew several sorts of liquors ... [including] *Uisquebaugh-baul* which at first taste affects all the Members of the Body: two spoonfuls of this last Liquor is a sufficient Dose; and if any Man exceed this, it would presently stop his Breath, and endanger his Life."

While the life-threatening properties of *usquebough-*

*baul* may have been exaggerated, the islanders' fondness for spirits meant less grain for food. Those who were resettled on the islands after the Highland Clearances of the nineteenth century were given tiny strips of infertile land to cultivate. Plenty emigrated or moved south. In Glasgow, so many would shelter from the rain under the arch of the Central Station it became known as the "Hielanman's Umbrella".

## DISTILLATION ON LEWIS

On Lewis illicit distillation was practised quite openly until 1827, but being so remote became a disadvantage once the blenders began to dominate the industry. Malt distilleries were an anonymous link in the supply chain, and if you were far-flung your costs were inevitably greater.

Of course, provenance really matters today, and anyone who can boast that they produce the only whisky on an island has a definite advantage. First among the new generation of offshore distillers was Harold Currie who founded Arran in 1995, almost 160 years since the island's last licensed distillery closed.

Mark Tayburn exported Lewis's first cask of whisky for 170 years from his Abhainn Dearg distillery in 2010. Five years later the Isle of Harris distillery was fired up as "a social distillery" with everything distilled, matured and bottled locally to maximize employment. "The population of Harris has halved in the last 50 years as the young migrate to the mainland," says the distillery's MD, Simon Erlanger. "So you've got an ageing population and a very fragile economy."

**BOTTOM LEFT** A fresh consignment of empty casks for filling at the Arran distillery.

**BELOW** Kenny Maclean, production manager at the new isle of Harris distillery in Tarbert, with some of the locals.

involved with the Dailuaine distillery on Speyside. Business soon picked up, as was clear from the regular coming and going of small steamers, or "puffers", arriving with grain and leaving laden with whisky. Unfortunately, the lack of a pier meant the casks had to be set afloat and towed three or four hundred yards out into the loch to be winched aboard. Despite increasingly desperate letters to the laird, Macleod of Dunvegan, the pier was only built in 1900. But Kemp had long since given up on Skye, selling out to his partner in 1892 and moving to the other side of Scotland where he bought Macallan.

## SAVED BY THE FIRE

For Robert Louis Stevenson it was a grand whisky – "The King o' drinks, as I conceive it, Talisker, Islay or Glenlivet!" Soon after that endorsement Talisker teamed up with Dailuaine, whose major shareholder was Talisker's manager, Thomas Mackenzie. The pair of distilleries was gradually acquired by the Distillers Company (DCL), who gained full control in 1925. Unlike

BELOW The functional, whitewashed buildings of Talisker are dwarfed by the distillery's dramatic setting, but its whisky is sufficiently robust and fiery to have been dubbed "the lava of the Cuillins".

most of its rivals, some Talisker was already being sold as a single malt, though most was being used in blends. It became a key filling in Johnnie Walker and had the brand's famous striding man logo on the label of its malts until the 1980s. This connection may have just tipped the balance when DCL accountants questioned the wisdom of keeping going such a far-flung distillery with all its added transport costs. Unlike Islay there were no sister distilleries on Skye to share the expense, and the bridge to the mainland was not built until 1995.

Some claim it was the fire in 1960, when spirit leaked out of one of the spirits stills and set the whole building ablaze, that saved Talisker. Having invested so much in the new still-house, its owners could not bear to close it down for good in the 1980s when the industry was drowning in surplus whisky. Yet probably more important was its inclusion in the original six Classic Malts in 1988. Its renown as a single malt took a while to catch on, but today it is hard to imagine that the distillery, which attracts over 50,000 visitors in a good year, was ever in danger.

One of the curiosities about Talisker is that it was originally triple distilled like an Irish whiskey. Today it has three wash stills supplying a pair of spirit stills and the strangest set of lyne arms in the whole of Scotland.

**BELOW** Today the far-flung beauty of Skye is an asset to the island's only single malt whisky, but in the days when almost every drop of Talisker disappeared into blends, its remoteness must have made the distillery feel quite vulnerable at times.

These are the copper pipes that connect the neck of the still to the condensers, or old-fashioned worm tubs in the case of Talisker, where the vapours are condensed into spirit. Instead of being straight, as at most distilleries, the lyne arms are contorted into a giant U shape which is connected to the still via something called a reflux pipe. Apparently up to 90 per cent of the vapour condenses back down this pipe to be redistilled.

Maybe the reason for this weird configuration was an attempt to replicate the old triple-distilled taste of Talisker, but no one really knows. What is true is that the cleansing effect of the extra copper contact that strips out impurities is offset by the inherent smokiness of the malt and the use of worm tubs, which tend to produce a heavier spirit. It all goes to make Talisker a truly unique single malt, and no one would dare tamper with any part of the production process. Its owners, Diageo, produce a range of ages, including the standard 10-year-old and the highly rated 18-year-old, of which all but one are bottled at 45.8 per cent abv. As with other popular single malts, growing demand has squeezed the supply of aged stocks and in response the distillery has released various expressions without age-statements like the recent Talisker Storm.

## WHISKY TASTING NOTES
### TALISKER STORM 45.8% ABV

Talisker has been bringing out a host of new expressions without age-statements, which might concern lovers of the superb 18-year-old, which has become harder to find, but there is nothing to worry about with Storm. The name pays tribute to Talisker's rugged location on the western side of Skye beside Loch Harport where things can get pretty stormy.

There is plenty of spice on the nose, ginger, and Talisker's signature peppery note with a thread of smoke. On the tongue this is a dense, richly textured dram with pronounced sweetness at first. On the back of the tongue comes the heat of the pepper as the peaty flavours come through. Adding water seems to underline the whisky's slightly salty edge.

# TOBERMORY ISLE OF MULL, ARGYLL & BUTE

Mull's capital Tobermory, with its pretty seafront of brightly coloured houses, was established in 1788 as a model village by the British Society for Promoting the Fisheries. Nine years later John Sinclair, a local kelp merchant, proposed a distillery, but the authorities suggested he build a brewery instead. Whether he simply ignored them or waited until 1823 when the distillery was officially registered is unclear. Either way Tobermory's current owners insist it began making whisky in 1798, making it one of the oldest commercial distilleries in Scotland still going. The date is embossed on every bottle of single malt.

**BELOW** Tobermory's stills, which were shut down in 2017 so they could be replaced, produced two distinct whiskies – the peated Ledaig single malt and Tobermory itself.

Sinclair leased a small area of land by the coast called Ledaig – Gaelic for "safe haven". In his first year he produced a paltry 292 gallons of spirit, possibly because he was still officially a brewer, or maybe because of his other business interests. He had a small fleet of vessels to ferry the kelp to Glasgow and Liverpool where it was used to make soap and glass.

PREVIOUS PAGE Tobermory's flagship 10-year-old and its sister malt – Ledaig – are fairly recent creations. For most of its history the distillery was at the whim of the big blenders, and spent much of the twentieth century in mothballs.

BELOW With its natural harbour, Tobermory was an ideal location for a new fishing village in 1788. Today its brightly coloured seafront has been popularized by the children's television series Balamory.

When he died in 1837, the distillery died with him in the first of many long siestas. In the words of Alan McConnochie, the former distillery manager: "Tobermory may have suffered from being run by enthusiastic amateurs."

Thirty years later in was back in production and, after a string of owners, passed to the Distillers Co. in 1916. It was a brief interlude however, for in June 1930 during the Depression, Tobermory shut down and remained so for 41 years. At first it would have been "mothballed" for better times ahead, but once the stills and washbacks had been ripped out, the likelihood of it ever making whisky again faded with each passing year.

In 1971, a consortium of "enthusiastic amateurs" performed an extraordinary act of resuscitation on Tobermory. Maybe they were seduced by its dreamy setting cradled beneath high cliffs across the bay from Scotland's most photographed waterfront. Or perhaps it was the size of the development grant. The venture soon failed, but by putting in new stills and washbacks and restoring the building, it was enough to rescue the distillery which was bought by Burn Stewart in 1993. With the burgeoning interest in single malts, especially from Islay, Tobermory's relatively remote island location suddenly became its core strength. And now with over two decades of uninterrupted production there are sufficient stocks for a raft of aged expressions either as "Tobermory", or its peated cousin – "Ledaig".

In 2013 Tobermory was purchased along with its sister distilleries of Deanston and Bunnahabhain, by the South African group – Distell. In early 2017 it was announced that whisky production would stop for two years while a new set of stills were installed.

# WHISKY TASTING NOTES
## LEDAIG 10-YEAR-OLD 46.3% ABV

Since it went back into full-time production after decades lying idle, the Tobermory distillery has had a split personality. It all revolves around peat, which is barely present in the eponymous single malt, but wafts out of its sister malt – Ledaig – pronounced Led-chig. Both whiskies have doubtless benefited from being bottled at a higher strength without the need to chill filter. With Ledaig the smoke is gentle and soft and perhaps more evident on the tongue than the nose, where there is also a vague hint of pine. In the mouth there is a definite malty richness that also comes from the wood, cut with some spicy flavours, possibly cloves and black pepper. There is a smoky mineral note on the finish.

# THE HIGHLANDS

"The Whisky of this county," wrote Robert Burns, "is a most rascally liquor, and by consequence, only drunk by the most rascally part of the inhabitants." His words, in a letter to an Ayrshire friend, date from a time when Scotland produced two very different types of whisky. There was the legalized stuff produced by licensed distillers in the Lowlands, and the illicit variety most associated with the Highlands. Burns was almost certainly referring to the former, which was pumped out on an industrial scale in large, shallow-bottomed stills at a fearsome pace. Up in the Highlands, which had yet to embrace the industrial revolution in any form, something less "rascally" would have been produced.

# THE WHISKY HERITAGE OF THE HIGHLANDS

The Wash Act of 1784 helped separate Highland and Lowland whisky by introducing different rules for distilling north or south of a line from roughly Dunoon to Dundee. It encouraged the big Lowland distillers to work their stills flat out, though most of their production was sent south for rectifying into English gin.

In recognition that life was tougher in the north, Highland distillers were allowed smaller stills and were exempted from the malt tax. However, to placate their Lowland counterparts, who feared unfair competition, no Highland whisky was supposed to cross the line.

Thus the Highlands became a whisky region, whose quality was allegedly better for being distilled in smaller pot stills and at a slower pace. As the government extended its authority northwards, stamping out smuggling en route, illicit Highland whisky began to flow south. Being illegal only added to its allure. As the Irish said of *poteen*, it was: "superior in sweetness, salubriety and gusto to all that machinery, science and capital can produce in the legalized way."

There was also a political dimension. After the Jacobites had been crushed at Culloden in 1746, Highlanders took to whisky as the spirit of defiance. While the Lowlands embraced the industrial revolution, and Edinburgh became a beacon of the Enlightenment, the Highlands slipped into a twilight zone until Sir Walter Scott rebranded it. His novels and epic poems created a tragic and romantic dreamscape that Victorian tourists found irresistible. Meanwhile the locals were heading in the opposite direction, lured by the prospect of jobs, or evicted to make room for sheep in the Highland Clearances.

Within this vast region, the Central Highlands – the broad sweep of land from Loch Lomond to Perth – was home to almost 130 licensed distilleries in the mid-nineteenth century. Add in all the moonshine being made, and the area was probably producing more malt whisky than anywhere else in Scotland. The smugglers enjoyed a good passing trade along the old drove routes to the big Lowland cattle markets.

## THE PERTH HUB

Only five distilleries survive and they are mainly clustered around Perth which became a major hub of the Victorian railways. It was also home to whisky blenders like Dewar's, Bell's and Matthew Gloag & Sons of The Famous Grouse. In the Western Highlands the cull of distilleries was even more dramatic, with just two survivors in Oban and Ben Nevis. Being in Fort William, an important garrison town must have helped Ben Nevis, while Oban was popular as "the gateway to the Isles".

As for the rest, many were simply too small to survive once local demand evaporated with a declining population, while the big blenders in Glasgow and Leith had access to malt whisky much closer to hand. On the East Coast barely a handful of more than 70 distilleries built in Angus and Aberdeenshire still remain. Aberdeen and Inverness were once thriving whisky towns, but their distilleries have all gone. Distilling has fared better beyond Inverness where there are nine distilleries still going, including two on Orkney.

Glengoyne, 14 miles north of Glasgow, just squeezes over the line and is therefore a Highland whisky like Pulteney in Wick – a good five hours away by car. The maritime malts of the West Coast are closer to the sweet, cereal Perthshire whiskies in distance, but poles apart in style, which just shows that the term "Highland" is not much of a signpost in the single malt jungle.

**LEFT** Old Pulteney in Wick, Caithness, can trace its distilling roots back to 1826 and its various brands have been regular award-winners.

87

# GLENMORANGIE TAIN, ROSS-SHIRE

Glenmorangie's stills are more feminine than the dumpy, onion-shaped ones you find in most distilleries and, at nearly 17 feet, their slender necks are the tallest in the industry. Glenmorangie now has 12 of them, apparently all modelled on the pair of second-hand gin stills from London bought by William Matheson when he first obtained a licence to distil whisky on his farm in 1843. The distillery grew out of an old brewery that he inherited when he took out a lease on the Morangie farm near Tain on the southern shores of the Dornoch Firth.

By the time the Victorian whisky writer Alfred Barnard visited 40 years later, Glenmorangie was producing 20,000 gallons a year. This was quite a feat for a distillery that he claimed was "almost in ruins", and "certainly the most ancient and primitive" he had seen. One suspects Barnard was doubtful the distillery would survive, which it has in spectacular fashion. Had he been able to travel through time and revisit the distillery today he would be amazed. His eyes would doubtless bulge at the sheer scale of the place, which hums with a relentless rhythm 24 hours a day, seven days a week – and would probably pop out of their sockets at the sight of the computer screen through which the entire distillation process is controlled by one man.

All this was way into the future, and would never have happened without the late-nineteenth-century boom in blended Scotch. This brought outside investment into the Glenmorangie Distillery Co. formed in 1887, and allowed the distillery's complete renovation before it collapsed altogether. Yet interestingly not all the whisky was sold to the blenders, for casks of its "pure Highland Malt" were being shipped as far as San Francisco. On seeing a consignment destined for Rome, the local paper speculated whether the Pope himself had requested "the Mountain Dew of Easter Ross", as it daintily referred to the whisky.

Production doubled after the rebuilding, and the distillery clung on through the boom-bust years at the start of the twentieth century. It limped through the First World War, when recruits from the Argyll &

Sutherland Highlanders were billeted in its malt barns, and was up for sale before the war was over. In April 1918 it was bought by Macdonald & Muir, a leading firm of blenders from Leith, for the princely sum of £74,100.

## BLENDS ACROSS THE SEA

New ownership brought security, for Macdonald & Muir had a number of popular blends like Highland Queen to soak up Glenmorangie's production of malt whisky, which was swiftly cranked up to 110,000 gallons a year. The barley mostly came from local farmers and was delivered to the malt barns near the entrance. From there the production process flowed downhill, for the barley to be steeped, then spread over floor maltings for a week and then dried over a peat kiln. Peat was used exclusively until the late 1940s, cut at first from the nearby Tarlogie hills, which have always been the source of Glenmorangie's water, and then from Orkney.

The worldwide slump sparked off by the Wall Street Crash of 1929 led to the distillery shutting down in March 1931 for five years. In the meantime the ending of Prohibition in the USA signalled a light at the end of the tunnel for firms like Macdonald & Muir. By the outbreak of the Second World War, almost four-fifths of all the whisky produced by the company was being shipped to America. Much of the US success was down to the firm's

**LEFT** American oak bourbon barrels waiting to be filled with Glenmorangie's sweet new-make spirit. After ten years most of the whisky will be bottled, but some will spend months, or even years, in a more exotic cask.

"Martin's VVO" blend, which included a good dollop of Glenmorangie.

By 1971 Americans were drinking 36 million cases of Scotch whisky a year – a threefold increase on 1960. The industry was in rude health and happily extrapolated past sales to predict future growth. Sadly, however, its US consumers gave Scotch the image of being "an old man's drink" among a new generation that had embraced vodka. As US sales declined, Glenmorangie began to explore other avenues. With William Grant's enjoying success with Glenfiddich, it was decided to start laying down stocks for a regular single malt.

It was a smart move and, by the late 1970s, such was demand for its 10-year-old malt, the company decided to cease floor malting and build a new still-room on the site. Within ten years, Glenmorangie had caught up with its great rival Glenfiddich in the UK, and was soon claiming to be the bestselling single malt in Scotland. The company became a PLC, though it remained in the control of the Macdonald family, and in 1997 bought Ardbeg.

### FINISHING SCHOOL

Since the 1920s the firm had also owned Glen Moray on Speyside, but with just three distilleries they needed to expand the repertoire of its flagship malt – Glenmorangie

RIGHT At just under 17 feet high, these are the tallest pot stills in the industry. Allegedly, they are modelled on the original pair bought by Glenmorangie's founder William Matheson from a Victorian gin distillery.

– to compete with larger rivals in the market. Dr Bill Lumsden, now the firm's head of distilling and whisky creation, was asked to come up with new expressions of the single malt. After a decade maturing in American oak, ex-bourbon barrels, the whisky was either bottled as the 10-year-old, or sent to "finishing school" to spend six months to a year maturing in different casks.

These included a port wood finish, a sherry cask finish and a Sauternes finish, which began to appear alongside the 10-year-old mother hen like a brood of chicks. Glenmorangie's expanded family spread across the supermarket shelves, displacing some of its rival malts completely – a perhaps not unintended consequence. A raft of other finishes came and went as Lumsden and his team pushed the concept to the limit, and while the mania for wood innovation may have subsided, it certainly boosted Glenmorangie's sales.

In 2004 the French luxury goods group Louis Vuitton Moët Hennessy gobbled up Glenmorangie PLC for £300,000 and gave the whiskies a luxurious makeover with prices to match. The bottles became curvaceous and new names were conjured up. Out went the prosaic-sounding port finish, which became "Quinta Ruban", while the Sauternes now glories in the title "Nectar d'Or".

## WHISKY TASTING NOTES
### GLENMORANGIE NECTAR D'OR 12-YEAR-OLD 46% ABV

If you can forgive the slightly pretentious name, Nectar d'Or is what was once known as the Glenmorangie Sauternes finish, or "extra matured" as they now like to call it. It comes from the standard 10-year-old pulled from its slumbers in ex-bourbon American oak barrels to spend up to two years "finishing school" in casks that previously held the famous sweet pudding wine of Bordeaux.

The result is a fabulously seductive, silky-smooth take on Glenmorangie's light, honeyed orange peel style. What comes through from the extra months is probably less to do with the cask's previous contents than the spicy quality of the European oak that complements the coconut sweetness of those old bourbon barrels.

# PULTENEY WICK, CAITHNESS

Huddled beside the North Sea, the small town of Wick can feel pretty bleak at times. It lies just eighteen miles south of Scotland's northern tip of John O'Groats, and apart from Dounreay, a few local serviceas and some inshore fishing there is not much work to keep hold of the young. Like other Highland outposts, Wick's population is shrinking slowly.

It is hard to believe, therefore, that this was once the great boom town of the north whose size was doubling every decade in the latter half of the nineteenth century. It was all down to the humble herring, for which Wick became the biggest fishing port in Europe – far larger than Hull or Grimsby, with a fleet of up to 1,000 boats. It was said that when they were all in port you could walk from one side of the harbour to the other across the decks, while the assembled masts would have been the closest thing to a forest in this part of Scotland. At the start of the fishing season, an army of workers descended on the harbour to gut the fish and pack them into salt barrels. The barrels were then loaded on to cargo ships to feed the insatiable demand for herring on the other side of the North Sea.

## THIRSTY WORK

The harbour was originally part of Pulteneytown, which faced its neighbour of Wick on the other side of the river. It was a purpose-built fishing village designed by the engineer Thomas Telford in the early 1800s, and commissioned by Sir William Pulteney MP, the first chairman of the British Fisheries Society. With fishing and gutting fish such thirsty work, James Henderson, who had been making whisky at his family home for some time, seized the opportunity with both hands.

He founded Pulteney in 1826 as an urban distillery in the centre of the community with its own captive market. The town's customs officers ensured there was no threat of competition from illicit stills, and there was easy access to other markets along the east coast and over the sea to Russia, Germany and the Baltic States. Not that there was any great need to export, given the scale of demand on the doorstep. According to one report from the 1840s, this modest fishing village was consuming a staggering 500 gallons (2,230 litres) of whisky per day. It seems Henderson could not have picked a better place.

His two stills were rudimentary and had a curious shape, assuming the current ones are modelled on them. They have a bulbous boil ball, like a huge Adam's apple beneath the neck, which is mimicked by Old Pulteney's bottle. They are hardly the most handsome stills in the whisky industry, and appear to have been sawn off at the neck as though to fit beneath the still-house roof. Today there is ample space for more elegant stills, but no one is thinking of changing the design now.

For as long as anyone can remember the whisky has been known as Old Pulteney, and was once "perfectly white", claimed the novelist Neil Gunn, recalling his childhood in the early twentieth century. It was consumed "on the quays of Wick more for its effect than its flavour", or so he said. If it really was colourless, they were either drinking new-make spirit fresh from the

LEFT By appearances Pulteney employed more folk than Glenmorangie and its famous "16 men of Tain" who were also invariably pictured with wooden shovels, known as shiels, used to turn the malt.

still, or the casks used were totally inactive.

By the outbreak of the First World War, Scotland's herring fleet was already shrinking thanks to the larger Scandinavian drift netters. The backlash against the demon drink had already started, and the town's 10,000-strong, seasonal workforce was blamed for all manner of depravity. In 1920 Henderson's descendants sold the distillery to James Watson & Co., a firm of blenders from Dundee. It was good timing on his part, for in 1922 Wick, along with 56 other towns in Scotland, voted to go dry and remained so for 25 years. It was the high water mark of the temperance movement when Edwin Scrymgeour, Britain's first and last prohibitionist MP, defeated Winston Churchill in Dundee in that year's general election.

## SPREADING THE NEWS

A few years later James Watson & Co. was swallowed up by the Distillers Company, who promptly closed the distillery down in 1930. It was not until 1951 that Robert Cumming, a local lawyer who had also acquired Balblair down the coast near Tain, cranked Pulteney back to life.

**BELOW** When Wick was a fishing boom town with a fleet of 1,000 boats and a huge seasonal workforce with an insatiable thirst for whisky, its resident distillery could barely keep up with demand.

It then passed to the Canadian group Hiram Walker, who effectively rebuilt it in the late 1950s, before they too were absorbed, this time into Allied Distillers. Finally, in 1995 Pulteney came to rest with its present owners Inver House Distillers, who gave this rather neglected, far-flung outpost of Scotch whisky some much-needed TLC.

As long as its malt production disappeared into blended Scotch, Pulteney was acutely vulnerable to the cycles of the whisky industry, particularly given its remoteness. Beyond the town and those in the business, the distillery was anonymous. That changed with the launch of Old Pulteney 12-year-old single malt in 1997 to mark the 50th anniversary of the repeal of prohibition in Wick. Inver House has drawn heavily on the whisky's maritime heritage: the way the barley and barrels were transported by boat and how the distillery workers were often fishermen as well. A fishing boat is etched on the bottle, and the brand has sponsored various seafaring endeavours. These have included Sir Robin Knox-Johnson's successful bid to sail solo round the world for a second time in 2007, and Jock Wishart's expedition to the North Pole by rowing boat four years later.

Inver House also restored an old herring drifter, the *Isabella Fortuna*, to spread the news of what it called "The Genuine Maritime Malt" up and down the coast, and gradually brought out older expressions up to and including a 40-year-old in 2012. There have also been a couple of non-age-statement whiskies named after the *Fortuna* and another herring drifter – *The Good Hope*. All this reflects a whisky that may not actually contain any salt, but does have a trace of sea spray on the nose to complement the sweeter, fruit and nut flavours on the tongue.

# WHISKY TASTING NOTES
## OLD PULTENEY 12-YEAR-OLD 40% ABV

The northernmost distillery on the Scottish mainland does a raft of older single malts and different expressions that play on wood like Navigator – a marriage of sherry and bourbon casks – but its flagship 12-year-old is a cracking whisky and pretty good value too. Swirled around in the glass, there is a pleasing fragrance that combines some tropical notes like bananas with a grassy aroma and maritime freshness. The coastal, far-flung setting of the distillery may well exaggerate the desire to find a salty note, but there is something there. On the tongue there is a gentle citrus fruitiness and notes of orange peel with a little caramel sweetness that gives it a nice, mouth-coating texture. The finish is lingering and dry.

# HIGHLAND PARK, SCAPA AND THE DISTILLERIES OF THE NORTH EAST

Highland Park on Orkney has long been the most northerly outpost of whisky making in Scotland. At the time of writing there is a bid to build a boutique distillery on Shetland, though previous plans to do so came to nothing. In the past there have been other distilleries on Orkney, including Stromness, but Highland Park and the much smaller Scapa are all that survive.

While the shortage of local grain may have dampened the supply of home-grown whisky, the need for a strong, heart-warming spirit on Orkney has been constant over the centuries, especially during the long, cold winter nights. Come the summer, visitors can bask in equally long hours of sunlight. Guests at the Castel Hotel in Kirkwall, Orkney's capital, used to be offered a dram and a slice of ginger cake whatever hour they arrived.

Highland Park stands just outside Kirkwall and the oldest buildings date from 1826, when Robert Borwick took out the first licence, although it has been claimed the distillery was founded as early as 1798. Illicit distillers were certainly operating in the area, including the local minister, Magnus Eunson, or so it was claimed. According to one

**RIGHT** Highland Park is one of just seven distilleries to have retained its floor maltings for part of its needs. Turning the malt twice a day using a traditional wooden shiel used to cause an ailment known as monkey shoulder.

story, he escaped being caught with whisky in his church by concealing it inside a coffin. The man who finally arrested him, John Robertson, is said to have taken over the distillery in a brief partnership with Borwick, whose family owned Highland Park until the 1860s. At that point the heir to Highland Park was Robert's youngest son – the Rev. James Borwick who, being a minister of the Kirk, felt compelled to sell the distillery for the princely sum of £450. It then passed through various hands until bought by James Grant, owner of the Glen Grant distillery on Speyside, who doubled the number of stills to four in 1898.

## HEATHER IS SWEET

By this point some Highland Park was being drunk as a single malt and had even reached the imperial courts of Denmark and Russia, though most was going into blends like Haig's and Ballantine's. The distillery did use a proportion of local "bere" barley – an indigenous, low-yielding strain that disappeared from the mainland, and heather which was laid on top of the peat in the kiln to offset the smoky bitterness. Visitors to the distillery were shown the heather house and then invited to inhale the pronounced sweetness that wafted up from the furnace. That practice died out long ago, and soon the grain was all coming from the mainland. However the distillery is still partly supplied from its own floor maltings and continues to use heathery sweet Orcadian peat, cut from the nearby Hobbister Moor.

By 1937 the value of Highland Park had increased to £185,000 – the price paid by Highland Distillers, which eventually became part of the Edrington Group. Having given its sister distillery Macallan a lavish makeover, they decided to do the same for Highland Park. The packaging was polished up, and a raft of one-offs and limited releases were unleashed to complement the core range of age-statements that begin with the 12-year-old. The marketing department has relied heavily on the islands' Nordic roots.

Meanwhile, after years on the endangered list, its neighbouring distillery of *Scapa* returned to full production in 2004 after a £2 million refurbishment by

**RIGHT** Orkney heather was once used by Highland Park according to the Victorian whisky writer, Alfred Barnard. He wrote that the heather was picked in full bloom in July and laid on the kiln to "impart a delicate flavour of its own to the malt".

Allied Distillers. Without this investment by the distillery's former owners, Scapa would have doubtless disappeared. It was founded in 1885 by the Glasgow blenders Macfarlane & Townsend, and passed to the North American distillers Hiram Walker in 1954. They rebuilt the distillery five years later and installed a Lomond wash still to produce a heavier, more oily spirit. Today the official bottling is the 16-year-old.

## MAINLAND MALTS

Back on the mainland, the first distillery after Pulteney is Clynelish, just by the coastal village of Brora, overlooking the Moray Firth. Its functional, box-shaped design dates from 1967 and belies the fact that there was a much older distillery here. The original Clynelish that you can still see was built by a Glasgow blending firm in 1896, replacing an even earlier version that was established by the Marquis of Stafford in 1819. The new Clynelish may look nothing like the original, but it aimed to produce a similar style of whisky with the same water source and same shaped stills. In 1969 the original distillery was fired up again under the name Brora, though a totally new malt whisky was created. Robust and heavily peated, it was a mainland version of Islay whisky which the distillery's owners needed for its blends. Heading south along the Dornoch Firth, near Glenmorangie, is Balblair, which was established in 1790 by John Ross. The distillery remained in family hands until it was sold to an Inverness wine merchant, Alexander Cowan, in 1894. The following year he rebuilt Balblair half a mile north beside the Highland railway line. By the outbreak of the First World War, Balblair had closed down and remained so until 1949, having been bought by a local solicitor, Robert Cumming, for £48,000 the year before. Then after a couple of decades with Allied Distillers, it was bought by Inver House in 1996. Despite having a whisky known only to blenders and an inventory full of holes, the new owners have carefully built up a reputation for Balblair as a single malt. Like Glenrothes, which may well have been the inspiration, the malts are sold in bulbous bottles by vintage stretching back to 1965. On the Black Isle near Inverness, Glen Ord is the sole survivor of a thriving cottage industry of farm distilleries. It was founded in 1838 by Robert Johnstone and Donald MacLennan, who went bankrupt within a decade. Various new owners took it on, until it passed to a firm of blenders in Dundee and finally to the Distillers Company (now Diageo).

The distillery is dwarfed by the neighbouring Glen Ord Maltings, which supply a fair number of local distilleries, but since 2007 it has built a loyal following for the Singleton of Glen Ord single malt in Asia.

## WHISKY TASTING NOTES
### HIGHLAND PARK 12-YEAR-OLD 40% ABV

Up on Orkney they have been embracing their Viking roots at Highland Park with expensive, limited-edition whiskies like Odin, Thor and Freya – the Norse Goddess of love. The distillery also does some lovely older whiskies including a gloriously rich and complex 18-year-old. However, the standard 12-year old sets the bar pretty high with its signature note of heathery peat that adds a real sweetness and sprinkling of spice to this fine dram.

The smoke drifts through to the palate, and adds a pleasing dryness to the richer malty flavours. Yet what you really notice is quite how polished and smooth this whisky tastes. Roll it round your tongue and see if you can pick up some of the dried fruit, peat and spice.

# CENTRAL HIGHLANDS AND THE WEST COAST

Distilling, legally or otherwise, was once endemic right across the Highlands from the perthshire glens to the west coast. today's survivors among those old nineteenth century distilleries are few and far between and, as isolated outposts of the whisky industry, they tend to have little in common.

Most of the old Perthshire distilleries closed long ago. Those that survived tended to be tied to a blend like Bell's and its long association with *Blair Athol*. Licensed in the late 1790s, this farm distillery struggled to compete with all the local illicit stills, until resuscitated by Alexander Connacher in the 1820s. Within 60 years he was supplying malt to Arthur Bell & Sons in Perth, who finally bought the distillery in 1933, even though it remained mothballed until after the war. Blair Athol's moment of glory came in the 1970s when the company trebled production in a bid to make Bell's Britain's top-selling blend. The reward for this achievement was a hostile, and ultimately successful, takeover bid from Guinness PLC, which eventually evolved into Diageo.

*Aberfeldy*, by contrast, was tied to Dewar's White Label

RIGHT Blair Athol; the spiritual home of Bells, which became the UK's top-selling Scotch whisky in the 1970s.

almost from the day it was established in 1898. According to family folklore it was near the croft from which the original John Dewar departed to walk to Perth, where he set up the family business in 1846. As well as an emotional bond there was sound commercial logic. Aberfeldy, on the banks of the Upper Tay, was connected by rail and had plentiful supplies of water. Having merged with arch-rival James Buchanan & Co. in 1915, the two firms became part of the Distillers Company. In 1998 Aberfeldy and its three sister distilleries were sold to Bacardi along with the Dewar's brand and Bombay Sapphire gin for an eye-popping £1.15 billion. Two years later Bacardi spent £2 million on turning Aberfeldy into the Dewar's World of Whisky, and while the distillery does produce a 12-year-old single malt, the focus is almost entirely on the Dewar's blend.

## BANDIT COUNTRY

A similar approach has been taken by the much smaller *Glenturret* distillery near Crieff, which became home to "The Famous Grouse Experience" in 2002. While Glenturret is the brand's spiritual home, its physical contribution to the blend in terms of malt whisky is small. To the south lies the last and most recent of the Perthshire distilleries, *Deanston*, housed in one of James Arkwright's late-eighteenth-century "satanic mills". The building only converted to whisky making in the 1960s.

Beyond Perthshire, on the way back towards Glasgow, is *Glengoyne*. Today as tourists flock northwards to the Trossachs, east of Loch Lomond, it is hard to believe this was once bandit country. It was full of cattle rustlers, like Sir Walter Scott's romantic hero Rob Roy, and whisky smugglers. Glengoyne was founded in 1833 by George Connell, right on the edge of the Highland line. Before long it was connected by rail to the big blending houses of Glasgow and Perth, and much of the malt began disappearing into Lang's Supreme, whose owners bought the distillery in the 1870s.

It was owned by the Lang Brothers for almost a century before coming into the fold of what became the

Edrington Group. As its key blend declined, Glengoyne found itself overshadowed by its new stable-mates Macallan and Highland Park. Since 2003 it has thrived as part of the much smaller independent whisky company Ian Macleod Distillers.

## WEST COAST

While the distilleries in the Central Highlands have been thinned out over the years, it is nothing to the cull on the West Coast. Since it was founded in 1794, out of what was originally a brewery, *Oban* has witnessed countless distilleries along the Argyll coast come and go. Today it appears small and rather quaint with its solitary pair of stills, and hemmed in by the town that has grown up around it. Oban was a tiny fishing village when brothers John and Hugh Stevenson established a boat-building yard, a tannery and finally a distillery. The Stevensons continued to make whisky for another two generations, though it was always a sideline to the family's other business interests.

Having passed out of family hands in the 1860s, Oban was acquired by a Mr J. Walter Higgin, who began slowly rebuilding the distillery in 1890, while continuing to make whisky there. By all accounts the malt was in strong demand from the blenders. Feeling constrained by lack of space, Higgin tried to burrow into the cliff behind the distillery to create a warehouse. In doing so he discovered

**RIGHT** Now well into its third century, Oban's distillery is almost as old as the town itself. Its survival is partly down to being chosen as the original West Coast whisky among Diageo's "Classic Malts".

a secret cave and the bones of a Neolithic tribe – these now reside in the National Antiquities Museum in Edinburgh.

Apart from the rebuilding of the still-room in the 1960s, Oban has changed little since Higgin's day and has been in pretty much continual production except for six years during the 1930s. As part of the Distillers Company, now Diageo, it may have felt vulnerable at times as a far-flung supplier of malt whisky for blends, but its future was secured the day it joined the original line-up of Classic Malts in 1988.

It is over an hour's drive north beside Loch Linnhe to the other long-established West Coast distillery of *Ben Nevis*. It was founded in the shadow of Britain's tallest mountain by "Long John" Macdonald in 1825. By the 1880s such was the demand for "Long John's Dew of Ben Nevis" that a second Nevis distillery with seven stills had been built alongside, which was merged under one roof in 1908. Beside whisky, there was a sawmill and a farm with 200 head of cattle fed on the draff from the distillery. There was also a small fleet of steamers and a total workforce of 230.

A century later, with the farm and steamers long gone, the name "Long John" resurfaced as a popular blended Scotch owned by Whitbread, who acquired the distillery itself in 1981. A decade later Ben Nevis was sold to its current owners – the Japanese drinks giant, Nikka.

## WHISKY TASTING NOTES
### OBAN 14-YEAR-OLD 43% ABV

This West Coast single malt from Oban – the gateway to the Isles – has been a proud member of the Classic Malts since the start, yet the distillery's solitary pair of stills have struggled to keep up with demand. There is just not that much of it available in bottle. The limited releases often reserved for duty-free are often worth seeking out, but the one constant has been the 14-year-old. There is a brisk, fresh quality to this malt, immediately apparent on the nose. It is only moderately peated, but the smoke with its aromas of iodine and brine mingles with vanilla oak. On the tongue the malty flavours come through, adding a richer flavour and pleasing texture.

# EDRADOUR PITLOCHRY, PERTHSHIRE

**When the big bosses of the whisky industry worry about overproduction, as they do every few decades or so, the last place they look is Edradour in the hills beyond the Perthshire town of Pitlochry. This dolls-house distillery is one of the smallest in Scotland, and with an annual production of 90,000 gallons, it produces what a reasonably big malt distillery might pump out in a week.**

Edradour was built in 1837 by a group of local farmers, including Duncan Forbes who had been distilling legally in these parts since 1825 and no doubt illegally before then. Plenty of moonshine was being made in these remote, tucked away hills with their abundant access to water. Today Edradour is the sole survivor among seven farm distilleries in the small parish of Logierait, and now belongs to the independent bottler, Andrew Symington. One of the lost distilleries was Ballechin whose name lives on in a heavily peated expression of Edradour.

Symington was inspired to launch Ballechin after reading Alfred Barnard's account in his monumental guide to Britain's whisky distilleries written in the 1880s. Travelling through the parish by open carriage, he wrote of "the rich treasures of beauty spread out before us" and of the burns "which are associated at every secluded bend and shady corner with the smuggling bothy." Like many a Victorian convert to the new vice of whisky, Barnard was clearly entranced by the drink's illicit past, describing the smugglers as men of "remarkable muscular power and shrewd audacity".

Back in 1933, the distillery which then belonged to the Macintosh family, was bought as a barely going concern by W. Whitely & Co. for £1,050. William Whitely was one of the more colourful rogues in the trade who survived bankruptcy to launch the King's Ransom blend in 1928. It was soon claimed to be the most expensive whisky on the market, and its US agent was none other than Mafia boss, Frank Costello. During

**OPPOSITE** Edradour is a classic, small-scale farm distillery that has barely changed since Victorian times.

Prohibition the brand along with its sister blend; The House of Lords, was smuggled into the States via the island of St Pierre, off the coast of Newfoundland.

Having made his own 'king's ransom' during Prohibition, Whitely passed the business to one of Costello's associates, Irving Haim who owned Edradour until he died in 1976. Six years later, the distillery was acquired by Pernod Ricard's then small whisky arm – Campbell Distillers who promptly opened it up to the public and in 1986 began bottling Edradour as a single malt, the first time its owners had ever done so. But the quantities produced were tiny and it never really fitted in with Pernod's growing portfolio of brands and distilleries. In 2002 it was sold to Symington who has preserved it as a thoroughly traditional distillery ever since.

Upstairs there was an old Morton's refrigerator that had been cooling the wort since the 1930s. When it

**BELOW** Edradour's pocket-sized mash tun is as old as the distillery itself.

finally packed in in 2009 most distillers would have replaced it with a modern heat exchanger, but not its new owners who insisted on an exact replica in stainless steel at considerable expense despite it having no tangible impact on the whisky. That one detail speaks volumes about Edradour's stubborn, some would say obsessive, belief in tradition.

The rest of the process, from fermentation in Oregon pine wash-backs to distillation in two of the smallest stills legally operating in Scotland, happens in one downstairs room. Jostling for space with a quaint-looking spirits still, is an open topped mash tun that is as old as the distillery itself. As well as being almost comically small, the mash tun is brightly painted in red and green like an old carousel from a fairground. Until recently four men would clamber inside, once the mash was done, to shovel the residue out through a hole in the wall. Health and Safety put a stop to that.

**ABOVE** It may be a dolls-house distillery, but there are undoubtedly smaller craft distillers than Edradour now operating since this sign was erected.

## WHISKY TASTING NOTES
### EDRADOUR 10-YEAR-OLD DISTILLERY EDITION 40% ABV

The house style at Edradour could be described as relatively sweet and fruity, thanks to the way the spirit is distilled and the fondness for ex-sherry casks since Andrew Symington took over in 2002. A year later he began creating a separate, heavily peated line called Ballechin, which may show its best in ex-Bourbon wood. There is also a wide range of malts that have been finished or fully matured in wine casks such as Barolo, Burgundy, Madeira and Sauternes. The Distillery Edition 10-year-old offers hints of dried fruit and sherried sweetness on the nose and a trace of fruitcake and golden syrup on the tongue, before a mellow, oaky finish.

# SPEYSIDE

Rising in the mountains south of Loch Ness, the River Spey flows north-east for 100 miles through Banff and Moray to the sea. The valley, known as Strathspey, may feel a long drive from the Central Belt, but this is nothing compared with how it was before the advent of modern roads and railways. Then this corner of Scotland felt far more remote, and through the long winter months it would close in on itself behind the vast granite bulk of the Cairngorms. When the tracks and unpaved roads were clogged with snow, it would have been virtually cut off from the outside world.

# THE WHISKY HERITAGE OF SPEYSIDE

Throughout much of the eighteenth century, this was an untamed wilderness for the government, while the locals survived on subsistence farming. In Speyside's higher glens it was better to distil any spare grain than try to compete with the fertile barley farms by the coast. There was no shortage of water for whisky-making, or peat to malt the barley and fire the stills.

As the authorities stamped out smuggling further south, the whisky of this region became more valuable, especially from one particular glen in Upper Speyside that specialized in moonshine. There were countless stills bubbling away in the remote hills above the river Livet, and word of its whisky even reached King George IV. On his famous state visit to Scotland in 1822, he demanded Glenlivet before he had barely stepped ashore. Elizabeth Grant of Rothiemurchus, wrote of how the Lord Chamberlain, "was looking everywhere for pure Glenlivet whisky," and of "emptying her petbin where the whisky was long in wood, long in uncorked bottles, mild as milk and with the true contraband goût in it."

In the early 1820s the region's distillers began to go legal, though production remained small-scale and seasonal, being an adjunct to the main business of farming. It was the advent of the railways that allowed Speyside whisky to flourish and supply the blenders in the late nineteenth century, yet the romance of those early bootleggers played a crucial role. Victorians loved the romance of the noble savage distilling in his cave surrounded by mountains and rutting stags – an image captured in Landseer's famous painting of the illicit still.

Glenlivet was probably the first real brand of malt whisky, though originally the name referred to the glen more than the distillery founded by George Smith in 1824. When the first blenders arrived they simply asked for Glenlivet, or at least whisky made in that style. Distillers throughout Speyside responded by bolting the magic G-word to their names.

In 1867 the Strathspey railway line opened with "whisky stations", such as Ballindalloch, Aberlour and Knocando. Distilleries sprung up beside the tracks with a siding to speed up the ebb and flow of grain and whisky. The trains brought coal and coke to heat the stills and malt the barley which in turn created a lighter, less smoky whisky which appealed to the blenders. Between 1886 and 1899 no less than 23 distilleries were built on Speyside, in the most dramatic building boom the whisky industry has ever known.

## BOOM TO BUST

But it went from boom to bust as World War I, US Prohibition and the Great Depression caused many Speyside distilleries to close or work sporadically. Distillers went bust, merged or were bought out, often by the ever-expanding Distillers Co, now Diageo. Today there are more than 40 distilleries on Speyside, way more than any other whisky region, and most are currently working flat out to supply's the world's newfound thirst for Scotch and especially single malts.

It was at Glenfiddich that the modern age of single malt whisky started in the 1960s. Successful malts like Macallan and Glenlivet rely on the power of their brand, rather than their provenance. For many of the others, it is hard to stand out as a Speyside single malt, and the region doesn't pack quite the same punch as Islay. It is also hard to talk of a definitive regional style beyond vague references to a heathery sweetness and little, if any, use of peat.

LEFT Thomas Telford's famous cast-iron bridge over the Spey at Craigellachie, built between 1812 and 1814, is still carrying pedestrians and cyclists. It was the advent of decent roads and railways that really opened up Speyside as a whisky region.

# GLENFIDDICH DUFFTOWN, BANFFSHIRE

As a distillery, Glenfiddich is well into its third century, having been founded in 1887; as the most popular single malt on the planet, however, Glenfiddich is a child of the 1960s. Then again, single malts barely existed before this independent Speyside distillery taught the world there was more to whisky than blended Scotch. It was in 1963 that it launched itself in its trademarked triangular dark green bottle.

The rest of the industry was faintly bemused, given the widespread belief that malt whisky was too robust a flavour to ever catch on beyond a tiny handful of drinkers. According to received wisdom, distillers existed for one reason only. Their job was to provide the base ingredients for blenders to turn into a smooth, consistent spirit to satisfy whisky drinkers from Seoul to San Francisco. Fifty years on, Glenfiddich has more than disproved that idea, and today you can drink the single malt made by virtually every malt distillery in Scotland whether bottled by the owners or by a third party.

All this was way into the future when William Grant took the plunge to start his own business and leave his job as a bookkeeper at Mortlach, the first distillery in Dufftown. When his original plan to open a lime works came to nothing in 1871, he returned to Mortlach, where another idea slowly began to take shape. He would build a distillery of his own, but it took 16 years to acquire the confidence and the necessary funds to do so. With a wife and nine children to support on an annual salary of £100, plus £7 as precentor at the Free Church of Dufftown, it was never going to be an overnight decision.

Glenfiddich was cobbled together from second-hand stills and equipment bought from Elizabeth Cumming, the lady distiller at what is now Cardhu. The distillery itself cost £650 and used stones dug from the bed of the River Fiddich, a nearby tributary of the Spey. The water to steep the barley and help make the spirit came from the Robbie Dhu spring, while a small burn provided the power for a malt mill.

The distillery somehow survived the great whisky crash at the start of the twentieth century, as well as the First World War and Prohibition in the USA. By the time William Grant died in 1923, much of the malt was being used in the company's own blends. The odd bottle even reached as far as Vancouver in one direction and Adelaide in the other. The self-sufficient, defiantly independent nature of William Grant & Sons survives to this day.

## THE GLENFIDDICH TRIANGLE

In the post-war years, the company had to compete against a rather overbearing Distillers Company who threatened to choke off supplies of grain whisky unless Grant's stopped supplying the big brewers with blended Scotch. Having installed its own coppersmiths and cooperage in the late 1950s, the firm built its own grain distillery at Girvan in 1963. By then the distillery

**BELOW** In 1969 Glenfiddich built a visitors' centre and threw open its doors to the public. At first the whisky industry was sceptical the idea would catch on, but more than half Scotland's distilleries have since followed suit.

was producing a 5-year-old whisky called Glenfiddich Pure Malt – a niche brand sold only in Scotland. This was replaced with an 8-year-old which was made available south of the border. From there it spread to duty-free and eventually the world beyond.

Glenfiddich's triangular bottle helped it stand out, and businessmen claimed to like the way it fitted into their slim, Samsonite briefcases. Others appreciated how it stacked easily in a cellar, while one woman, possibly with tongue in cheek, praised the way it didn't roll out of bed like other bottles. At first the sales team found it difficult to persuade hotels and bars to stock a single malt, since no one had ever asked for one. Yet in terms of price and packaging it was really sold as an alternative to deluxe blends like Chivas Regal and Johnnie Walker Black Label. Because these were 12-year-old whiskies, Glenfiddich soon found it had to raise its age accordingly.

Those marketing Glenfiddich in the early days were

**BELOW** Glenfiddich claims that it is the only Highland whisky to be bottled at source and use the same water throughout the process.

certainly inventive. Seeing that actors invariably drank cold tea instead of Scotch when having a dram on stage, it was decided to bottle a line of the whisky with flat ginger ale. It certainly beat yesterday's PG Tips, and soon bottles began to appear in London's West End, giving the brand some much-needed free publicity.

In 1969, Glenfiddich pioneered the idea of whisky tourism by throwing open its doors to the public for free, and encouraging them to spend money in the visitors' centre and distillery shop. Again the Scotch whisky establishment was sceptical that anyone would want to look round a factory, yet before long there were plenty of similar distillery visitor centres.

With its cooperage, copper-smithy and bottling hall surrounded by endless warehouses, Glenfiddich is a hive of industry. Its 29 stills pump out sufficient spirit for a current annual production of 1.1 million cases of single malt spread over a core range of age-statements, including 12, 15, 18 and 21-year-old, and a raft of special editions. Among the rarest expressions have been the 55-year-old Janet Sheed Roberts Reserve. She was William Grant's last surviving granddaughter – and Scotland's oldest woman when she died in 2012 aged 110.

## WHISKY TASTING NOTES
### GLENFIDDICH 15-YEAR-OLD SOLERA RESERVE 40% ABV

The name Glenfiddich may be slightly tarnished for malt whisky aficionados, if only because of the tall poppy syndrome – the main expression is ubiquitous and the distillery itself is huge. But there is a lot more to Glenfiddich than its light, grassy 12-year-old that gave so many whisky drinkers their first taste of single malts.

The main ingredient is 15-year-old whisky from ex-bourbon barrels, but some is aged in virgin oak and some in sherry casks. All three are then tipped into a Solera vat, the sort you might find in Jerez, and married together. The result is an orange-scented, lightly sherried whisky with some sweet spice, raisins and fruitcake.

# GLENLIVET BALLINDALLOCH, BANFFSHIRE

"The single malt that started it all" is how Glenlivet sees itself. The glen in question in Upper Speyside was famous for its illicit stills. According to one local farmer, "There were not three persons in Glenlivet in those days [in the early 1800s] who were not engaged directly or indirectly in the trade." In late autumn after the harvest, when the smuggling bothies were most active, the sweet scent of distilled spirit must have filled the air. The glen came to define a style of whisky well before anyone spoke of Speyside as a whisky region. Indeed so famous was the word "Glenlivet" that a trail of distilleries almost to the coast bolted its name on to theirs in the hope of some reflected glory.

**BELOW** In 1824, George Smith took out the first distiller's licence in the parish of Glenlivet. After struggling with hostile neighbours and near bankruptcy, he became one of the most successful distillers in Scotland.

The Glenlivet distillery ought to have been flattered, though in truth its rivals were really using the glen with a small "g" as a generic type. It wasn't that they wanted to be mistaken for the whisky-making venture of George Smith who became the first licensed distiller in these parts. In 1822, when every drop of whisky in the glen was moonshine, no less a figure than King George IV was asking for some Glenlivet when he arrived in Edinburgh on his famous state visit. It was the first time a British monarch had set foot north of the border since 1650 and the whole event was stage managed by Walter Scott. Swathed in tartan, with his gouty legs wrapped in pink tights, "the portly Hanoverian" might seem almost comic, as though auditioning for a part in a forerunner to *Brigadoon*. Yet the Scottish establishment took him very seriously indeed, and began to embrace the romanticism of the Highlands.

## A WARM WELCOME

Two years later, in 1824, George Smith obtained a licence to make whisky at his farm of Upper Drummin which had been leased from the Duke of Gordon by his father. Within three years the new venture was on the brink of bankruptcy and Smith had to go cap in hand to the Duke's factor. In return for abandoning the lease on a neighbouring farm and selling off his cattle he received a £500 rescue package. At the time he was being routinely intimidated by all the illicit distillers in the glen, who didn't take kindly to the new Glenlivet distillery. As Smith wrote of his venture: "I was warned before I began by my civil neighbours that they meant to burn my new distillery to the ground, and me in the heart of it." Not surprisingly he made sure he always carried a pair of hair-trigger pistols that he had been given by a local laird.

By 1830 most of the smugglers and moonshine operators had either been flushed out of the region or had been encouraged to take out a licence. Before long, Smith was selling his Glenlivet malt to blenders in Aberdeen, Perth and the Port of Leith. Among his customers was Andrew Usher, the man dubbed "the father of blended Scotch". In 1853, Usher launched his pioneering "Old Vatted Glenlivet". Today it would be

**BELOW** Compared to Glenfiddich, Glenlivet was slow to join the single malt revolution, but it has long been the most popular malt in America and may yet overtake its arch-rival.

designated a blended malt, since it did not contain grain whisky like Usher's Green Stripe and the plethora of blends that followed.

The distillery moved down the glen to its current home to be nearer to the newly opened Strathspey railway line. Production jumped to 4,000 gallons a week and the casks were taken by horse and cart to Ballindalloch station. Smith became a minor celebrity among distillers, with newspapers keen to know about him, and by the time he died in 1871, Glenlivet was clearly the best-known distillery in Scotland. It was said that over 100 casks a year were being sold in London, though it is unclear whether the malt was blended up by publicans and grocers or served in its original form. In 1882 George Smith's heirs managed to reduce the number of distillers piggy-backing on their name to just 10 after a costly two-year tussle in the courts.

**BELOW** Having moved his distillery down the glen from Upper Drummin, George Smith sent his whisky by cart and then train on the Strathspey line. Soon Glenlivet was producing up to 4,000 gallons a week.

Glenlivet would have been the obvious contender to lead the great malt whisky renaissance in the 1960s. Indeed it could have done so 80 years earlier, being the only vaguely recognizable brand among single malts. Instead it was left to Glenfiddich, while Glenlivet spent the sixties selling most of its malt to blenders, in common with Glen Grant and Longmorn, with which it had merged as a limited company. The one exception was the USA, where Glenlivet has long been the bestselling single malt. It was a market first developed by Bill Smith Grant after Prohibition, when the distillery started to bottle some of its own whisky instead of selling it all in cask.

In 1977 Glenlivet and its sister distilleries were bought by Seagram's, whose key focus was the Chivas Regal blend. Then, in 2001 Seagram's spirits division was carved up, with most of the whisky going to the French group, Pernod Ricard. Its single malt sales climbed to over 600,000, pushing Glenlivet up to second position behind Glenfiddich. In 2010 a £10 million expansion was announced, adding six stills to the existing 14 and boosting the overall capacity by 75 per cent. Glenfiddich's days in pole position may be numbered.

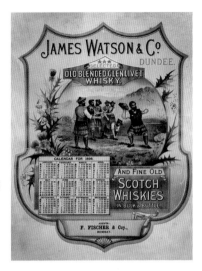

**ABOVE** The name Glenlivet was widely used by whisky blenders like Watson's of Dundee. Initially it would have been a blend of malts until it included grain whisky. How much actually came from the Glenlivet distillery as opposed to the region in general is unclear.

# WHISKY TASTING NOTES
## THE GLENLIVET XXV, 43% ABV

This gold-medal-winning whisky is one of the super premium whiskies produced by George and JG Smith. After 25 years' maturation in cask, the final couple of years are spent in specially selected ex-Oloroso sherry butts, which adds an extra dimension of dried fruit, orange, dark chocolate and a crème brûlée sweetness to the floral, honey and candied fruit found on the original spirit. This is a rich and opulent dram with a warming cinnamon spice note and very definite hints of Christmas cake with its dried fruit and nutty elements. The finish is long and satisfying with ginger and a creamy orange edge to the balanced finish. A warm and satisfying whisky for a cold winter's evening.

# THE MACALLAN CRAIGELLACHIE, BANFFSHIRE

In January 2014 a six-litre Lalique decanter of Macallan M, one of only four produced, became the most expensive whisky ever sold at auction. The whisky had been selected from seven sherry casks, the oldest dating from 1940, and the final price when knocked down by Sotheby's in Hong Kong was a jaw-dropping US$628,205. Two years earlier a bottle of The Macallan 50-year-old appeared in the James Bond movie Skyfall. It was no mere product placement, like the bottle of Heineken which features for a brief moment earlier in the film. In its scene Macallan plays an almost starring role.

It has been quite a journey for what began as a humble farm distillery that first obtained a licence in 1824. Its founder was Alexander Reid, a tenant farmer who took out a lease on Easter Elchies farm on the west bank of the River Spey, a mile from Craigellachie. Reid had doubtless been selling moonshine to the drovers who would pass by on their journey to the big cattle markets of the Central Belt. They would pause for a while, buy a little whisky and then cross the river at a nearby ford.

It was originally known as the Elchies distillery, and by 1880 production had climbed to around 40,000 gallons a year. By then it belonged to James Stewart, a grain merchant who teamed up with three local bankers, including William Grant and Robert Dick, to raise funds. He planned to expand Macallan and build a second distillery – Glenrothes in the nearby town of Rothes – but it seems he became overstretched.

In 1892 Macallan was bought by Rodney Kemp, a self-made man with plenty of experience in the drinks trade, having been a wine merchant in Elgin and a partner in the Talisker distillery on Skye. Six years later William Grant and Robert Dick had become founders of Highland Distillers, and now they made an unsolicited bid to buy Macallan. Kemp was unimpressed with their offer of £80,000 and it was not until almost a century later that Highland Distillers finally managed to acquire

Macallan in 1996. By then the price of the distillery had risen to £180 million.

Kemp disposed of his wine business to concentrate on the distillery, restoring the buildings, improving the equipment and boosting production to 2,500 gallons a week. By the time of his death in 1909, Macallan's whisky was well regarded by the blenders, but as a single malt it was all but unknown.

The distillery remained in family hands for most of the twentieth century, initially through Kemp's sons-in-law, first Alexander Harbison and then Samuel Shiach, who took charge in 1938.

Throughout this time the distillery had barely changed since the end of the nineteenth century, except for an additional pair of bonded warehouses. A little Macallan seeped into the States during Prohibition, but the home market shrank by a third. Somehow production kept going apart from the 1932–33 season

LEFT Macallan has cleverly maintained its premium, well-crafted image, despite the burgeoning scale of production. By 2014 it boasted 21 stills, and has since announced a £100 million expansion plan.

during the Depression and for a year during the Second World War. Gordon Shiach, an intelligence officer who had interrogated Hermann Goering at the Nuremberg trials, took over the distillery in 1947, but was killed in a road accident the following year.

## DON'T LOOK NOW

In the 1950s the distillery was rebuilt with a new, glass-plated still-house and there was a steady expansion of warehouses with one built every year. By 1970 production had hit one million gallons, by which point some casks were being set aside for a single malt. In 1978 the first bottles of Macallan 10-year-old were released, though not too many people heard about it. The firm had only started advertising in 1974 with an annual budget of £25, though a bottle of Macallan did appear in Nicolas Roeg's classic film *Don't Look Now* released the year before.

Its screen appearance on a bedside table in a Venice hotel room was fair enough given the scriptwriter was Allan Schiach, who combined his role as chairman of Macallan-Glenlivet with writing screenplays. Yet it is doubtful many in the audience noticed the whisky, given what was happening on the bed between Julie Christie and Donald Sutherland.

RIGHT A traditional dunnage warehouse showing some 500-litre sherry butts in the foreground. Sherry wood was once insisted on for all Macallan's malts, but that rule has been quietly dropped to allow bourbon barrels as well.

Macallan's use of Glenlivet in its title was common practice among Speyside distilleries, but this was quietly dropped as the distillery built its reputation for its single malt. Being relatively quick off the mark in the burgeoning malt whisky market, gave it a head start. Today it rivals Glenlivet for second place behind Glenfiddich in terms of sales of single malts.

One of the great cornerstones of Macallan's quality, part of its DNA, was the insistence on sherry casks to mature the spirit. Yet clearly bourbon casks were being used for some time as well, to allow the distillery to launch its Fine Oak range in 2004. More recently Macallan's owners, the Edrington Group, took the radical step of dropping age-statements for its new 1824 series which starts with "Gold" and "Amber" and rises in price to "Sienna" and "Ruby". Macallan has always insisted the colour of its whiskies is entirely natural, with no spirit caramel added.

Dropping age-statements was at least partly to cope with demand for its aged whiskies. For years production has been trying to catch up. In 2008 it expanded the number of its "famously small stills" to 21 at a cost of £20 million. Then, in 2014, it announced plans for a further £100 million expansion, due for completion by 2017.

## WHISKY TASTING NOTES
### THE MACALLAN SIENNA 43% ABV

Rather than use age-statements to differentiate its various expressions, Macallan has taken a bold and somewhat controversial decision to use colour, although in some markets like the US you can still find the classic 12-year-old. Because the whiskies are natural shades with no spirit caramel added, the colour reflects the condition of the cask – how active it is, and how long the spirit spent in it. Sienna sits above "Gold" and "Amber", but below "Ruby".

As the colour suggests, there is a real dried fruit richness which is there on the nose along with cloves, ginger and candied orange peel. On the tongue the fruit becomes obvious, with notes of figs and Christmas pudding as well.

# CRAGGANMORE BALLINDALLOCH, BANFFSHIRE

John Smith, who founded the Cragganmore distillery in 1869, was said to be the illegitimate son of George Smith of Glenlivet. Whether that was true or not, the man had Speyside whisky in his blood by the time he embarked on his own distillery, having been manager of Glenlivet and Macallan followed by a spell as the leaseholder at Glenfarclas before the Grant family took over in 1865.

**BELOW** The Cragganmore 12 year-old has the floral elegance of a classic Speyside, albeit with more depth and complexity.

Around this time Smith persuaded his landlord, Sir George Macpherson-Grant, to lease him a plot of land at Ballindalloch where he founded Cragganmore, which means "great rock" in Gaelic. It was close to the newly opened Strathspey railway line that ran from Dufftown to Abernethy where it connected with the Great North of Scotland Railway. John Smith was a true railway buff and quickly built a siding connecting his new distillery to the track so grain could flow in and whisky could flow out.

The venture prospered, and before long Smith had moved into a smart Scots-baronial house complete with a turret and crenulations. He loved travelling by train, but had to do so in the guard's van, since he could not squeeze his 22-stone bulk in through the carriage doors, even sideways. By the time of his premature death in 1886, the so-called whisky express, carrying up to 16,000 gallons of Scotch whisky in cask, was a regular feature rattling along the Strathspey line.

## KEEPING IT IN THE FAMILY

Cragganmore was producing 90,000 gallons a year when Gordon Smith inherited the distillery from his father. Most of its whisky was sent south to the Dundee blending firm of James Watson & Co. that eventually became part of the Dewar's empire.

By 1901, having barely missed a fortnight's production since inception, Smith decided the distillery needed rebuilding and hired Charles Doig – the leading distillery architect of his day. His design with the compact, whitewashed courtyard is what you see today.

## UNIQUE STILLS

The two wash stills which feed the pair of spirit stills are unique in the industry. They appear to have been sawn off at the neck, with their lyne arm, which carries the vapours to the worm tubs, jutting out like a branch. No one knows whether they were specially designed to fit the original space, but they clearly work.

New-make Cragganmore has a robust, almost Highland character which matures into one of the more complex Speyside malts. It was always well regarded by the blenders, and in 1988 was picked to represent Speyside in the original line-up of the "Classic Malts".

PREVIOUS PAGE
Cragganmore had always been in demand from blenders as one of the more complex Speyside whiskies around, and there was no surprise when it was picked to represent the region in the original line-up of the six "Classic Malts".

# WHISKY TASTING NOTES
## CRAGGANMORE 12-YEAR-OLD 40% ABV

When it was decided to launch the Classic Malts to represent the whisky regions, Diageo's predecessor was spoilt for choice when it came to Speyside. The choice of Cragganmore was a good one and the 12-year-old has stood the test of time. It has the floral elegance of a Speyside, but a real depth and complexity too.

The nose manages to combine the fresh scent of cut grass and herbs with honey, nuts and baked fruit, as well as some sweetness from the American oak. On the tongue it has a soft, rounded texture and some ripe fruit from the malt, and you might pick up a very faint wisp of smoke on the finish.

# GLENROTHES

Every year the Speyside town of Rothes produces the equivalent of fifty million bottles of single malt, though of course the vast majority of it disappears into blends, which is one reason why the town appears coy about its main industry. Of its four distilleries, the most hidden – tucked down a leafy gorge beside the Rothes burn – is Glenrothes.

Its founder, James Stuart, was looking to build something bigger and better than Macallan, the small farm distillery he had owned since 1868. He found what he was looking for in a disused sawmill with a nearby spring to supply water, and the burn to supply power via a waterwheel. Work began in 1878, the year Britain was plunged into the worst financial crash for almost a century. His partners, Robert Dick and

Willie Grant, worked for the Caledonian bank and had borrowed heavily from it. With the bank on the verge of collapse, they suddenly found themselves in charge of Glenrothes as Stuart decided to return to Macallan.

The new venture only survived with financial help from a local farmer, a retired rear admiral and the Presbyterian minister from nearby Archiestown who lent the distillery £600. Within five years Glenrothes was turning a profit supplying the Glasgow-based brokers and blenders – Robertson & Baxter. In 1887 it was decided to merge with Bunnahabhain on Islay and form the Highland Distillers company. For over a century, until it acquired Macallan in 1996, Glenrothes, or "The Heilan" as it was affectionately known, was the jewel in the company's crown. Since then Highland Distillers has become part of the Edrington Group.

**OPPOSITE** As a key filling for popular blends like Cutty Sark and Famous Grouse, it seemed there was never any Glenrothes to spare to lay down casks for a single malt. That finally changed in 1994 with the release of the first Vintage Malt.

**BELOW** In keeping with this generous spirit, miniatures of Glenrothes come double sized.

In 1900, Glenrothes was producing 300,000 gallons from its four stills, and remained in almost continuous production until 1933 despite a dramatic fire the previous decade which sent a torrent of flaming whisky into the Rothes burn. People flocked to scoop up the escaping nectar, and the trout had never been so easy to catch, according to the local paper.

As a key component in Cutty Sark and other brands like Famous Grouse, almost every drop of Glenrothes was swallowed up by the blenders until 1994 when a limited amount was released as a vintage malt through Berry Brothers & Rudd in London. This venerable wine and spirit merchant owed its fortune to Cutty Sark – the blend it created in 1923. In recent years Berry Bros. has taken control of the Glenrothes single malt in return for giving the Edrington Group Cutty Sark.

OPPOSITE Glenrothes by night when all you can hear is the muted thrum of machinery and the babbling of the Rothes burn.

# WHISKY TASTING NOTES
## GLENROTHES 2001 43% ABV

Joining the single malt revolution a little later than most, Glenrothes decided on a different tack. Rather than produce standard age-statement whiskies like a 10- or 15-year-old, Glenrothes chose to select casks from a particular year when the spirit had reached full maturity and release it as a vintage. The 2001 is an interesting play on wood, probably mainly ex-bourbon barrels with some sherry butts as well, though the recipe remains secret. On the nose there is lemon sherbet, some honey, some freshly cut wood and some baked fruit from the malt. The taste has a zesty citrus character with vanilla ice-cream and a hint of that raisin sweetness you find in PX sherry. In a word it's beguiling, exotic and hard to resist.

# GLEN GRANT ROTHES, BANFFSHIRE

One of Glen Grant's claims to fame is that this distillery is unique in being named after its founding family. John and James Grant had been partners in the Aberlour distillery when they founded Glen Grant in Rothes in 1840. John Grant was a distiller, while his brother was an engineer and local politician.

**BELOW** Glen Grant boasts the best landscaped gardens of any distillery, and a walk along the burn where Major Grant kept his whisky safe is a must.

Within a year of opening their new venture the Grants began lobbying for the Elgin to Craigellachie railway to be extended via Rothes. In the end they helped bankroll the new line with a £4,500 cheque in 1858. For years Glen Grant remained the only distillery in Rothes and in 1872 passed to John Grant's nephew, James Grant, who was universally known as "the Major". When not driving around in the Highlands' first

ABOVE AND BELOW Sporting the best mutton-chop whiskers on Speyside, John Grant (above) was succeeded by his nephew (below). Major James Grant was the classic Victorian gentleman distiller with a penchant for big-game hunting in Africa and salmon fishing on the Spey.

registered motorcar like a Scottish "Mr Toad", he could be found flogging the Spey with his fly rod or big-game hunting in Africa. He returned from one safari in what is now Zimbabwe with a young boy he had found abandoned by the roadside. It seems the boy, who was rechristened Biawa, had been orphaned after a tribal feud and "the Major" decided he would be better off in Rothes. He went to the local school, became a lifelong supporter of Rothes FC and allegedly even played for them in goal occasionally.

Back in 1898, such was the success of Glen Grant that it was decided to build another distillery across the road with copies of the original stills. The prosaically named Glen Grant No.2 boasted a whisky pipe above the traffic that connected it to its mother distillery like an umbilical cord. The pipe was something Customs & Excise insisted upon, but it ran dry four years later. The new distillery did not reopen until 1965, when it was rechristened Caperdonich. It closed in 2002 and was finally demolished in 2010. The Major died in 1931, having outlived all but one of his eight children. His grandson Douglas Mackessack took over and became one of the last "gentleman distillers" in Speyside. In 1977 he bowed to commercial pressure and sold Glen Grant to Seagram, who had long been using its malt in

Chivas Regal. The new owners set about restoring the distillery's famous gardens, where Major Grant used to take guests for a moonlit tour after dinner. They would pass conservatories full of orchids and exotic fruits, walk across lawns bordered by rhododendrons and majestic copper beach trees and continue up a path beside a burn. The party would stop by a gorge where the Major would unlock a small safe embedded in the rock to produce glasses and a bottle of Glen Grant. While the conservatories have gone, the gardens and the whisky safe remain.

Together with the distillery the gardens and whisky safe attract thousands of visitors, many from Italy – a connection that goes back to 1961. That year an Italian entrepreneur, Armando Giovinetti, looked round the distillery on holiday and asked to buy a cask of whisky from Douglas Mackessack who probably thought he was mad. Yet Giovinetti got Glen Grant as a 5 year old single malt into the top hotels in Milan and Rome, and from there it became the top-selling whisky bar none in Italy. Today Glen Grant is owned by Gruppo Campari.

PREVIOUS PAGE In 1961 Armando Giovinetti, began importing casks of Glen Grant to Italy for bottling as a single malt. Within 20 years it had become the country's biggest-selling whisky.

# WHISKY TASTING NOTES
## GLEN GRANT 10-YEAR-OLD 40% ABV

The single malt from this Speyside distillery was always best known in Italy. For years its very gentle, straw-coloured 5-year-old was the country's most popular Scotch whisky of all, and you would find bottles of it behind virtually every bar. Since 2005 Glen Grant has been owned by Campari, the Italian spirits giant. Older, rarer expressions have long been available from independent bottlers such as Gordon & MacPhail. The standard 10-year-old bottled by Campari acts as a delicate, grassy, toffee-scented introduction to Speyside. It may not be the most complex single malt but it is balanced and well made with a soft, baked apple and cut grass flavour and a relatively short finish.

# CARDHU

John Cumming had been busted for smuggling whisky many times and had a string of convictions to prove it. It was probably his wife, Helen, who actually made the whisky at Cardow farm, which he leased in 1811. There were folk tales of how she would treat the excisemen to tea in her kitchen while her husband hoisted a red flag in the yard to warn anyone nearby with an illicit still.

In 1824 Cumming took out a licence, and though it remained a small-scale farm distillery at least the whisky could now be transported openly rather than be smuggled over the hills. On his death in 1846 the distillery passed to his daughter Elizabeth and her husband. When widowed in 1872, she became the first lady distiller on Speyside. Fifteen years later she sold the original stills to William Grant for his new venture

**ABOVE LEFT** John Cumming of Cardow, looked every inch the gentleman farmer, far removed from his grandfather's moonshine roots. Cardow was sold to John Walker & Sons, but he still ran the distillery.

**ABOVE RIGHT** Elizabeth Cumming, the first lady distiller on Speyside, re-equipped Cardow with new stills. The old pair were sold cheaply to William Grant, who installed them in his new distillery of Glenfiddich.

at Glenfiddich, and drew up plans for a new distillery. According to the whisky writer Alfred Barnard, the buildings were "of the most straggling and primitive description and although water power existed, a great part of the work was done by manual labour". Cardow was rebuilt in 1893 and then sold to John Walker & Sons on condition the family would continue running it. Most of the production was sent for blending, though there were early adverts for Cardow as "a single whisky". Elizabeth's son John Cumming took over, and by the 1920s had ensured that all the distillery workers' cottages had running water, electric light and even indoor toilets. Meanwhile the distillery continued to supply Johnnie Walker and other blends of the Distillers Company, whose chairman was later Sir Ronald Cumming, Elizabeth's grandson.

After a pause in distilling during the Second World War, production was cranked up to meet the surging demand for Johnnie Walker. The distillery became the spiritual home of the brand, though its physical contribution was small, especially once Cardhu's 12-year-old single malt took off in Spain. The Spaniards enjoyed it as a fashionable alternative to Chivas Regal – the country's top-selling deluxe blend. With sales growing by 100,000 cases a year from 1997 to 2002, demand was set to outstrip supply. Rather than raise the price to restrict demand, Cardhu's owners Diageo rechristened the brand Cardhu Pure Malt and blended in malts from neighbouring distilleries. In doing so they provoked a very public spat in the media, cries of betrayal and even questions in the House of Commons. Unleashed from the constraints of being fed from a single distillery, Cardhu could have become the world's most popular malt within 10 years. This fact was not lost on William Grant & Sons, owners of the top-selling malt at the time, Glenfiddich. Together with other distillers they forced Diageo into a humiliating climb-down and Pure Malt was quietly withdrawn from the market in March 2003.

## WHISKY TASTING NOTES
### CARDHU 18-YEAR-OLD 40% ABV

There has never been a great deal of Cardhu to spare for bottling as a single malt, due to the seemingly inexorable growth of the Johnnie Walker brand. Cardhu, or Cardow as it was known until 1980, was bought by John Walker & Sons as far back as 1893, and it has been used in its blends ever since.

The official 12-year-old was replaced with the notorious Cardhu Pure Malt in 2003, but reintroduced two years later. More recently there have been a number of older expressions released including this sumptuous, relatively full-bodied 18-year-old that appears to have quite a sherry influence. There is some old leather, macerated fruit and dark chocolate, though still some freshness too.

# GLENFARCLAS BALLINDALLOCH, BANFFSHIRE

On a meadow beneath the bare, wind-blasted bulk of Ben Rinnes lies the family-owned distillery of Glenfarclas. To have remained independent while virtually every other Scottish distillery is in corporate hands is quite an achievement. Over the years there have been unsolicited offers to buy Glenfarclas, but the Grant family are resolutely not selling.

**BELOW** Glenfarclas has remained fiercely independent and wary of partnerships since its last one with the Pattison brothers of Leith went disastrously wrong in 1899.

John Grant took over the tenant farm in 1865 and a small distillery valued at £511 that Robert Hay had founded some 30 years earlier. Grant, a champion breeder of Aberdeen Angus cattle, was probably much more interested in the land than in making whisky. Yet as the demand from the blenders grew for Speyside malt, distilling became more important. The firm of J&G Grant was founded and it was decided that the distillery needed rebuilding. To raise the money a partnership was formed with one of the leading blenders – the Pattison brothers. When Pattison's went spectacularly bust in 1899, Glenfarclas was lucky to survive. The experience seems to have put the Grant's off outside investors for ever. Some "Pure Old Glenfarclas-Glenlivet" malt was bottled, yet the vast majority went for blending. The whisky baron Tommy Dewar was so moved by Glenfarclas he declared it contained: "The hum of the bee, the hope of Spring, the breath of May ..." and much else besides. In 1925 John Dewar & Sons were paying 6s.3d. a gallon for the whisky, as were John Walker & Sons. With the rest of the industry contracting around it, Glenfarclas must have felt vulnerable until it could establish a name for itself among whisky drinkers through its own single malt. In 1973 much of the distillery was rebuilt into what you see today, with a central hub of buildings

**BELOW** There is nothing dainty about the bulky stills at Glenfarclas, but then there's nothing dainty about the whisky either.

surrounded by row upon row of low, old-fashioned, dunnage-style warehouses. That year a visitors' centre was also installed. People traipsed beneath the pagoda roof into a reception room whose panelling came from an old luxury liner, the *Empress of Australia*, that was being scrapped. With its years of uninterrupted production and no city investors to placate, Glenfarclas has the luxury of boasting one of the best inventories of aged whisky in the business.

The standard line-up starts with a 10-year-old and progresses right though to the 40-year-old. But for the cask-strength 105 bottling, all the whiskies are in the same-shaped bottle and carry similar labels. What matters to Grant's is the liquid inside rather than any fancy packaging, and by today's inflated prices for rare, old whisky, the 40-year-old is something of a bargain. The style is not dissimilar to the original sherried whiskies of Macallan.

**OPPOSITE** A few years after Glenfiddich, Glenfarclas opened its visitor centre in 1973 and used panelling from an ocean liner, the Empress of Australia that was being scrapped at the time.

# WHISKY TASTING NOTES
## GLENFARCLAS 105 – 60% ABV

Having very nearly disappeared in the great Pattison crash at the end of the nineteenth century, Glenfarclas has been determined to plough its own furrow as a fiercely independent, family-owned whisky company. From its big, chunky stills flows a spirit that may not be the most subtle on Speyside, but it makes up for it with its generous, full-bodied charm. The 105 is one of the most well-established cask-strength whiskies around, and an undiluted dram is the liquid equivalent of a great bear hug. The full spectrum of sherry aromas waft out, starting with some dusty malt, followed by stewed plums, burnt sugar and chocolate. The palate continues the chocolate theme with more sweet spice from the wood, until eventually this big beast of a whisky fades to a slow finish.

# BALVENIE DUFFTOWN, BANFFSHIRE

It may have taken William Grant decades to realize his dream of having his own distillery of Glenfiddich in 1887, with every penny scrimped and saved, but it took him just five years to embark on his next project at a cost of £2,000. The new distillery was a conversion of the eighteenth-century Balvenie New House, and its stills were fired up on 1 May 1893.

**BELOW** William Grant's Balvenie is something of a boutique distillery within the grounds of the mighty Glenfiddich which has expanded greatly since the 1960s.

The decision to build Balvenie was taken partly because Grant had secured a valuable customer – a blender in Aberdeen – from the Glenlivet distillery, which was temporarily closed due to a fire. There was also the fact that a local man had been making enquiries about leasing land next-door to Glenfiddich to establish his own distillery. Had he succeeded he would have been entitled to half of Glenfiddich's precious water supply. To limit the expense, Grant bought his stills second-hand from Lagavulin on Islay and the now defunct Glen Albyn in Inverness. On hearing of a mash-tun for sale that might be too deep, he sent a terse note to his son, dispatching him to take a look. "Don't be afraid of the depth of the mash-tun if otherwise suitable," he wrote. "A man does not need to piss his pot full unless he likes."

At the start of the twentieth century William Grant & Sons was almost brought down by the bankruptcy of the Pattison brothers, one of its main customers. Afterwards it began to focus on its own blends, including "William Grant's Finest" and "Standfast". William Grant died in 1923 and years later one of his daughters-in-law wrote the following about a night-time visit to the distillery: "We would go to the still-house first. There Alfie Mackray, the night still-man, would be making his supper – not a carried

**BELOW** Like others, Balvenie has been very inventive with maturation. Its "Triple Cask" range involves ageing in first-fill Bourbon barrels, refill casks and first-fill Oloroso sherry butts.

'piece' but a nice, yellow haddock grilled to a turn on a shovel over a clean fire – the furnace fire, and a can, not a flask of tea ..."

The fish suppers may have gone, but Balvenie hasn't lost its old-world charm, having retained its floor maltings for a proportion of its malt, so smoke still billows from its pagoda roof. In addition Balvenie remains solidly late Victorian, while thrusting, modern Glenfiddich has expanded all around it. Balvenie eventually released its own single malt in 1973 wrapped in black leatherette and stamped with gold lettering. Quite who it was aimed at is unclear, but the packaging has sobered up since then, and the focus is now very much on wood to emphasize the crafted nature of Balvenie, which still has its own cooperage. As well as the popular Double Wood, there have been releases based on first-fill bourbon barrels, port pipes, rum casks and sherry butts. In 2014 two European oak casks were selected by Balvenie's malt master, David Stewart MBE, for release as a 50-year-old with an eye-popping price tag of £26,000 a bottle.

**OPPOSITE** Head south from the bustling whisky town of Dufftown, and the scenery grows increasingly dramatic. Before tarmac roads and railways, the region would quickly become cut off behind the granite bulk of the Cairngorms in winter.

# WHISKY TASTING NOTES
## BALVENIE 12-YEAR-OLD DOUBLE WOOD 40% ABV

The sister distillery and neighbour to Glenfiddich in Dufftown on Speyside is a very different creature. Balvenie has always been more of a boutique distillery with a loyal following for its finely crafted malts. Double Wood is about taking the malt matured for ten years in ex-bourbon American oak barrels and finishing them in sherry butts, for two years in this case. The richer sherry character may come through more on the tongue and give the whisky its fine creamy texture and add some dark fruit, sweet spice and chocolate to the flavour. On the nose there are some confected fruit aromas, possibly bananas and freshness too. The finish is fresh and tangy.

# CAMPBELTOWN

Cut off from the rest of Scotland at the end of the A83 way down the Mull of Kintyre, it seems highly improbable that Campbeltown was ever a centre of whisky making. Yet in its heyday towards the end of the nineteenth century, this small port was pumping out more whisky than any other region in Scotland. Today it seems more of a postscript, albeit with the highly regarded independent distillery of Springbank, the great survivor along with Glen Scotia of the worst distillery cull in the country's history. The relentless rise of Campbeltown whisky may have carried with it the seeds of its own demise, but its fall from grace was swift and brutal.

# THE WHISKY HERITAGE OF CAMPBELTOWN

Unlike the Highlands with its tradition of farm stills, Campbeltown was an epicentre of urban distillation once dubbed whiskyopolis. The town at the end of the Kintyre peninsular – the great arm of Argyle that slips into the Irish Sea, was once home to at least 34 distilleries.

Before the late Victorian boom on Speyside, Campbeltown was producing more whisky than any Scottish region. In 1914, 18 distilleries were in business but, by 1929, only the long-forgotten Riechlachan was still operating. If not for the survival of Springbank, and Glen Scotia's reopening in 1934, Campbeltown whisky would have ceased to exist.

St Columba is said to have sailed here from Ireland in the sixth century before progressing to Iona, so maybe he brought with him the secret of distillation. There was mention of *acquavytie*, or spirit, being delivered to the village of Taylone, 15 miles from Campbeltown, in the late sixteenth century, while in 1609 the first license to produce whisky here was granted to John Boyl. The timing was good for that same year the *Statutes of Icolmkill* had decreed that the Western Highlands should stick to home-made liquor and desist from imported wines and spirits.

There was plenty of barley and water, and other distillers soon followed. By 1713 whisky-making in Campbeltown was such that the Town Council appointed three inspectors to ensure no-one was producing

RIGHT The calm waters of Campbeltown Loch would have once been disturbed by an endless flow of spirit, but almost all the town's distillers disappeared thanks to the early twentieth-century whisky slump and US Prohibition.

watered-down spirit. In 1791 a hike in the license fee effectively drove Campbeltown whisky underground, and in the following three years excisemen seized no less than 292 stills in the town. But within a decade of the 1823 Excise Act the number of licensed distilleries leapt to 30. They quickly began shipping whisky across the Firth of Clyde to Glasgow, then the fastest-growing city in Britain.

Campbeltown distilleries came and went, but by the 1870s the numbers had settled on around 20. Before or since, there has never been such a concentration of distillers in one place. They had coal from nearby Machrihanish and malt from twenty local maltsters, while the grain was now coming from the Lowlands, Ireland and even Denmark and Russia. The draff was reportedly shipped to Rotterdam to feed the horses of the German Army. As an editorial in the local paper put it: "There is no saying where Campbeltown whisky ends, or what it sets in motion as it flows along, but the volume ... [is] enough to cause a navy as well as men's heads to swim."

## WATCHING THE SPIRIT FLOW

In 1886, with production running at more than 2.6 million gallons, Campbeltown's 2,000 inhabitants were said to have the highest income per capita of any town in Britain, while its whisky barons built themselves opulent villas. From here they could watch the endless flow of spirit to the blenders in Glasgow. But there were rumours, perhaps propagated by other whisky regions, that the town's distillers had grown complacent and were even using old herring barrels to store their whiskies. Meanwhile the big blenders were beginning to favour the lighter, heather-honey malts of Speyside.

However, the real reasons for the decline of Campbeltown stretched further. There was the industry-wide slump in the early 1900s, the war, US Prohibition and the Depression. When the industry finally recovered it was very different, and the town's myriad independent distilleries no longer fitted in. Yet three have survived including the iconic Springbank to keep Campbeltown whisky firmly on the map.

# SPRINGBANK AND CAMPBELTOWN'S OTHER SURVIVING DISTILLERIES

## KINTYRE, ARGYLL & BUTE

**In 1828, Campbeltown got its 14th licensed distillery in the shape of Springbank. It was built on the site of some old malt barns in the centre of town that belonged to Archibald Mitchell.**

As a maltster supplying all the new distilleries that were springing up, Mitchell was evidently making whisky on the side, judging by the ledger of a local firm of coppersmiths who were supplying him with the necessary kit. The Springbank distillery was actually established by his in-laws – the Reid family – but they soon found themselves in financial difficulties and the distillery was taken over by Archibald's two youngest sons, John and William Mitchell, in 1837. Within a year the reputation of the whisky had spread as far as Kilmarnock and a young grocer called John Walker who bought a quantity for 8s.8d. a gallon. It was a nice early endorsement from the man who would eventually lend his name to the world's best-selling Scotch, although the amount he paid when adjusted for inflation wouldn't even cover the duty today.

**RIGHT** Long before today's whisky anoraks began bagging remote distilleries, there was Alfred Barnard. During the 1880s he visited every single one of them for his seminal work: The Whisky Distilleries of the United Kingdom.

At some stage the brothers fell out over their other activity, sheep farming, and William Mitchell left to become a founding partner in Rieclachan – the town's last distillery to close for good in 1934. He later went on to establish Glengyle in 1872, by which point the extended Mitchell family had interests in four distilleries. Of these, Springbank, which traded under the name J&A Mitchell & Co. Ltd, was by far the largest.

When the Victorian whisky writer Alfred Barnard visited Campbeltown in the 1870s he wrote that "in former times the only trade of the place was herring fishing, net making and smuggling". By the time he got there it was definitely a one-industry town with 21 distilleries, all of which he visited. Having waxed lyrical about Hazelburn, the town's biggest distillery, he descended on Springbank with his notebook in hand. Every detail from the capacity of each washback, to the diameter of the boiler, and the horse-power of the steam engine was duly recorded, including the distillery's annual output. This was put at 145,000 gallons of "Campbeltown Malt" which was "principally sold in London and Glasgow". Barnard then progressed to Dalintober, Benmore and a host of other long-lost distilleries. There is not the slightest hint that Springbank might be one of the very few survivors.

**ABOVE** Barnard would have been amazed that so many Campbeltown distilleries disappeared, and that Springbank was one of just two survivors. With its direct-fired stills and floor maltings it remains one of the most traditional.

## SURVIVAL INSTINCT

More remarkable is the fact that Springbank has remained in the same family's hands since 1828, longer than any other distillery in Scotland. Yet that same sense of grim determination to remain independent when ownership of almost the entire industry is now shared by a few corporate players, may be a clue to its survival. Above all Springbank is a remarkably self-contained operation from start to finish. The original floor maltings are used to malt the barley, while the spirit is matured in the distillery's own warehouses on site. Even the bottling of the finished whisky is done at Springbank.

All this is relatively recent. Back in the 1980s Springbank was buying in its malted barley and sending its whisky off for blending like virtually every malt distillery in Scotland. Having just the one distillery down the far end of the Kintyre peninsula, left the firm of J&A Mitchell particularly vulnerable to any downturn in the industry. With their warehouses full of whisky in search of a home, the big blenders lost interest in the early 1980s. They were too busy closing their own distilleries to worry about buying in outside stock. Springbank desperately needed to control its own fate, and would have perished but for the great malt renaissance pioneered by Glenfiddich in the 1960s. If single malt was to be the saviour, the methods used were to be as traditional as possible. In 1992, the family decided to restore the old floor maltings and fire up the kilns with peat from Tomintoul. At the same time they determined that no more fillings would be sold to blenders, and to expand Springbanks's repertoire of malts under the names of Hazelburn and Longrow – two of the town's erstwhile distilleries. Hazelburn is triple distilled from unpeated malt and then part matured in sherry casks in the case of the 12-year-old, while Longrow is double distilled and distinctly smoky. Springbank sits neatly in the middle with moderately peated barley that is distilled two and a half times.

By 2000 Springbank had developed something of a cult following among single malt enthusiasts, and Hedley Wright decided to buy the distillery next door, founded by his ancestor William Mitchell in 1872. But for an empty shell there was not much left of Glengyle, which had not produced a drop of whisky for eighty years. Two second-hand pot stills were bought from Ben Wyvis – a malt distillery within the giant Invergordon grain distillery. After some slight modifications to improve the reflux, or copper contact between the spirit and the still, a lightly peated whisky was produced under the name Kilkerran.

It could not be called Glengyle because that name belongs to Campbeltown's third surviving distillery – Glen Scotia. Originally called Scotia it was established in 1832 by Stewart Galbraith & Co. Alfred Barnard wrote that it "seems to have hidden its way out of sight, as if the art of making Whisky, at that time, was bound to be kept a dark secret". In 1930, the then owner Duncan MacCallum threw himself into Campbeltown Loch after a dodgy business deal went wrong. His ghost still haunts the still-room, or so they say.

After a brief spell with the Bloch brothers, who cannot have found Campbeltown too convenient, given their other distillery was on Orkney, Glen Scotia eventually ended up with Glen Catrine (Loch Lomond Distillers) in 1994. It had undergone a £1 million refurbishment in the 1970s, but had spent many of the subsequent years in mothballs. Having brought the two stills back to life, the new owners have managed to bring out various aged expressions including a 12- and a 14-year-old despite the gaping holes in the inventory. The distillery has long been in the shadow of Springbank, but maybe it will start to emerge now that the parent company, Glen Catrine, has been bought by a private equity company as part of a management buy-out.

## WHISKY TASTING NOTES
### SPRINGBANK 15-YEAR-OLD 46% ABV

The great survivor down in Campbeltown and one of the few independents left in the industry, Springbank has a loyal following among malt whisky aficionados. The distillery rewards its fans with consistently good bottlings, setting the bar high with its entry level 10 year old. The house style is generous, robust and slightly salty. This older expression is a big beefy whisky with a distinct sherry influence. The nose is complex and offers candied fruit, toffee, coconut and some exotic sweet and sour spice. On the tongue the toffee and dried fruit notes continue, but this is balanced by dry spice, a little sea spray and some smoke as well. Adding a drop of water seems to smooth out the texture and enhance those fruit flavours.

# THE LOWLANDS

Distilling was once as endemic in the Lowlands as it was in the Highlands. There were a handful of big, commercial distilleries pumping out whisky at a ferocious pace, and endless illicit stills operating everywhere from remote farmsteads to inner-city tenements. The risk of being caught may have been greater than in the Highlands and Islands, but access to the market and good-quality grain would have been much better. Yet thanks to improved transport those benefits have faded, and other marketable qualities like having a romantic location have come to the fore. Today the Lowlands dominate grain whisky production, but malt distilleries are few and far between.

# THE WHISKY HERITAGE OF THE LOWLANDS

Over the past 150 years trains, planes and automobiles have made Scotland far more accessible. Today you can drive the 200-odd miles from Edinburgh to Ullapool – the gateway to the Outer Hebrides – in a little more than four hours. Once it would have been a huge journey and best avoided in winter when snow and ice would have often blocked all routes to the north.

**BELOW** A poster from 1937 advertising what was then Britain's favourite Scotch. Today the brand is probably best-known for its recently launched Haig Club grain whisky that is promoted by a certain David Beckham.

Besides there was little incentive to stray far from Edinburgh – that beacon of the Enlightenment – and venture into the twilight zone of the Highlands with its feudal chieftains and warlike clans. The Highland boundary fault, which is visible from Space, signified a cultural fault-line as well. In the Lowlands, the agricultural revolution was transforming the land and boosting yields dramatically. More grain per acre meant more whisky for the Lowland whisky barons like the Steins.

Andrew Stein built the Kennetpans distillery near Alloa in around 1720, and founded a whisky dynasty which included the Haigs and stretched to Dublin where John Stein established what became home to Jameson's whiskey. The family also owned the giant Kilbagie distillery, also near Alloa, which began sending vast quantities of raw spirit to England for rectifying into gin. In retaliation, London distillers choked off supply, causing the Steins, whose five distilleries were responsible for half the legalized whisky in Scotland, to go bust. The Haigs fared better and at their Cameronbridge distillery, Robert Stein installed Scotland's first continuous still in 1828.

Not all Lowland distilling was done on an industrial scale, and there were more than 200 licensed distilleries by the end of the eighteenth century, the vast majority producing malt whisky in small pot stills. There was also plenty of illicit distillation, though it was obviously harder to escape detection than in some distant

Highland glen or hidden among the reeking lums, or chimneys, of Edinburgh.

## ECLIPSED BY OTHER REGIONS

Towards the end of the nineteenth century other regions gradually eclipsed Lowland whisky. The big blending houses looked first to Campbeltown, and then Speyside, to provide most of their needs. A century later, when distilleries began to promote their own malts led by Glenfiddich, the Lowlands slipped further into the shade. Single malts were perceived as the spirit of the Highlands and Islands, where each whisky reflected its rugged and remote setting. But in terms of quality there were always some beautiful Lowland malts produced by distilleries such as St Magdalene and Rosebank.

Both the above fell victim to the whisky loch when scores of distilleries were closed in the 1980s and early 1990s. Those in the Central Belt were always more vulnerable to being bulldozed into history than some Highland distillery tucked down a remote glen. But the Falkirk distillery of Rosebank, dubbed the "King of Lowland whiskies", is currently being resuscitated by Ian Macleod Distillers who bought it in 2017. It will join those other 19th century survivors – Auchentoshan, near Glasgow, and Glenkinchie, near Edinburgh. There is also Bladnoch, in Dumfries which began producing again in 2017. Added to which are the new boutique distilleries planned or already in production like Kingsbarns in Fife and Clydeside in Glasgow

Also one mustn't forget the vast quantities of grain whisky distilled in the Lowlands in Girvan in Ayrshire, Strathclyde in Glasgow, North British in Edinburgh and the giant Cameronbridge in Fife. Add their entire production together and it would easily eclipse all the malt whisky produced in Scotland. And not all the spirit disappears into blends, as demonstrated by Diageo's new, David Beckham-endorsed Haig Club whisky in its fancy blue bottle. It may be coy about its provenance, but every drop of this single grain whisky is distilled at Cameronbridge.

# GLENKINCHIE PENCAITLAND, EAST LOTHIAN

When John and George Rate took up distilling whiskey on their East Lothian farm in 1825, they did not have to look far for their raw ingredients. The rich alluvial soil makes this prime barley-growing country, and there was water from the Kinchie Burn to make the mash. With a burgeoning market in Edinburgh just fifteen miles away, the small distillery appeared perfectly placed. There was even a railway direct to the city centre whose tracks ran just a few hundred yards from the distillery. But something happened causing the Rates to sell up in 1853.

**BELOW** All malt distilleries have a locked spirit's safe through which new-make spirit flows. When initial foreshots come through, the middle cut is collected and feints are rejected.

Then came the boom in blended Scotch, and with demand spreading to England and beyond, the prospects for Glenkinchie began to look up. As readers of the *Wine Trade Review* discovered in 1886: "The future of the wine trade is whisky." Up in Edinburgh it seems they already knew that, for five years earlier a consortium of various wine merchants and a local

brewer decided to set up The Glen Kinchie Distillery Co. The stills were fired back into life to provide malt for the blends, particularly Haig's Gold Label and Dimple. The distillery was later licensed to John Haig & Co.

The new owners completely rebuilt Glenkinchie into what you see today – a relatively substantial, four-storey distillery in red brick. It has a functional, somewhat municipal feel about it, but it was clearly efficient. In no time its pair of old pot stills, among the biggest in the industry, were pumping out almost 80,000 gallons of spirit a year. This was filled into casks and then dispatched via a siding onto the railway

**BELOW** Behind its red brick façade, Glenkinchie was one of the most modern and heavily automated distilleries in the country.

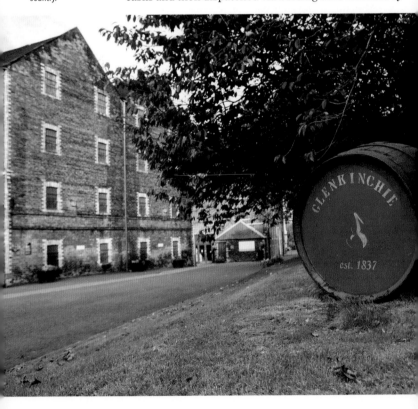

line to Edinburgh. The distillery even had its own overhead railway system to carry the grain to the floor maltings. Once malted, it was crushed in the grist hopper and transported by a mechanical elevator to a mash tun complete with mechanically powered rakes. By comparison with a typical Highland malt distillery at the time, Glenkinchie was positively space-age.

In 1914, it became part of a group of Lowland malt distilleries that was swallowed up by the Distillers Company after the First World War. During the next war, Glenkinchie was almost unique in being allowed to continue distillation every year, albeit at a much reduced rate. In 1969, the old floor maltings were converted into a museum, which may have played a small part in its owners' decision to pick the distillery to represent the Lowlands in its original line-up of six Classic Malts launched in 1988. The other contender was Rosebank in Falkirk whose whisky was possibly more esteemed, so maybe Glenkinchie was lucky to survive.

Being the closest distillery to Edinburgh it receives a steady stream of visitors from the capital.

PREVIOUS PAGE Every malt distillery has a locked spirit's safe through which the new-make spirit flows. Once the initial foreshots have come through, the distiller starts to collect the middle cut before rejecting the feints at the end.

## WHISKY TASTING NOTES
### GLENKINCHIE 2000 DISTILLER'S EDITION 43% ABV

If you have spent too long on Islay, and been seduced by its hairy collection of peat monsters, Glenkinchie might seem rather tame and perhaps, to some smokeheads, not even whisky at all. The counter argument might be that this Lowland distillery south of Edinburgh is all about subtlety and nuance. Better still, people should try this Distiller's Edition malt which has been rounded off at the end of maturation in Amontillado sherry casks, and decide for themselves. It has Glenkinchie's classic lightness of touch and dry grassy aroma, sweetened with the sherry oak. The palate is brisk and dry with a big hit of malt that fades to a lingering finish.

# AUCHENTOSHAN CLYDEBANK, WEST DUNBARTONSHIRE

Scotland's other main Lowland distillery lies close to the Clyde, some ten miles downstream of Glasgow. It was founded in 1800 by the village of Old Kirkpatrick and seems to have been originally known as Duntocher before it became Auchentoshan. Back then it was open country, whereas today the fields have been swallowed up by the urban sprawl of Glasgow and its suburbs spreading westwards.

**OPPOSITE** Auchentoshan is part of a stable of Scotch whiskies including Bowmore, Ardmore, Glen Garioch and Teachers owned by Japanese company Beam Suntory.

The first mention of "Auchentoshan" – meaning "corner of the field" – is from 1649 and refers to a monastery that would have been dissolved the previous century. The monks would have almost certainly brewed their own beer, and if they went further and distilled it, then the roots of whisky making here may be very old, though this is pure

conjecture. What we do know is that Auchentoshan was like a small Highland farm distillery, and in a similar way only took out a licence in 1825 after a good two decades of making moonshine. It was first owned by a man named Thorne, who was followed by the Filshie family and then the firm of CH Curtis in Greenock. It was they who showed Alfred Barnard round on his great distillery tour of the 1880s. In his book, Barnard describes Auchentoshan as a "little distillery ... situated in a romantic glen with a stream of water running past it". He adds that "at the time of our visit the haymakers were busy in the fields connected with the Distillery and consequently the Works were almost abandoned."

From a whisky point of view what sets Auchentoshan apart is the fact the spirit is triple distilled like Irish whiskey. A middle still sits between the wash and the spirit still to help separate the heads and tails and produce a cleaner, more refined spirit. Triple distillation gives you a lower yield and a higher alcoholic strength. People have speculated that Auchentoshan was simply playing to Glasgow's large Irish population who wanted a taste of home. On the other hand, triple distillation was once remarkably common in Lowland distilleries lying far from any Irish community. During the Clydeside Blitz, on 13 March 1940, the Luftwaffe scored a direct hit on one of Auchentoshan's warehouses causing the loss of 53 butts of whisky. In the 1980s, having been owned by various brewers including Tennent's, it was sold to Morrison Bowmore, who in turn were swallowed up by the Japanese drinks giant Suntory. Now that Suntory own Jim Beam, Auchentoshan sits in the same stable as Teachers, Ardmore, Glen Garioch and Bowmore.

**OPPOSITE:** Auchentoshan made headlines in 1941 when one of its warehouses received a direct hit from a bomb during the Clydeside Blitz, sending a flaming stream of whisky into the river. The bomb crater was later turned into the distillery pond.

# WHISKY TASTING NOTES
## AUCHENTOSHAN THREE WOOD EDITION 43% ABV

As one of just two survivors among old Lowland malt distilleries, Auchentoshan produces a light, grassy whisky which is made even more gentle through triple distillation in the Irish style. On to this pale canvas is painted a riot of sherry flavours in "Three Wood" which involves maturation in ex-Oloroso and Pedro Ximenez casks, as well as some American oak bourbon barrels. There is lots of dried fruit and burnt sugar on the whisky's fragrant nose, which gives way to a syrupy, mouth-filling palate. There are flavours of dried figs, raisins, dark chocolate and toffee which continue to the finish, though whether you can really taste the subtle distillery character of Auchentoshan beneath that sherried oak is a moot point.

# PART THREE

# WHISKY CULTURE AND TRADITIONS

# BURNS NIGHT AND HOGMANAY

Burns Night, as everyone knows, is whisky night – a bacchanalian feast to celebrate the national bard's birthday on 25 January. As one dram lurches into another in an unsteady procession of toasts, a poor, defenceless haggis is sacrificed – its belly slashed open to reveal its "gushing entrails bright". This being a line from Burns's address "to a Haggis" which is always recited in rousing tones by the master of ceremonies as he wields the knife.

In 1801, five years after Robert Burns died, a group of his friends met in the cottage where he was born in the Ayrshire village of Alloway for the first ever Burns supper. With haggis, poetry, singing and doubtless plenty of whisky, the evening was a great success and the friends decided to make it an annual event. A year later merchants in Greenock hosted the first Burns Club supper, and the idea was quickly adopted by other West Coast towns with a connection to the poet.

By 1806 Burns Night had reached Oxford University and four years later London. It then spread overseas when Scottish army officers celebrated the first Burns supper in India in 1812. Similar haggis and whisky-fuelled celebrations were reported in Canada, and before long the night had become a regular fixture in the calendar for ex-pat Scots throughout the Empire. In the furthest-flung tea estate or jute mill they may have struggled to find a haggis every year, but the drink was surely always whisky.

The combination of whisky and haggis is no accident. Haggis is made from sheep's pluck (heart, liver and lungs), minced up with oatmeal, spices and suet, wrapped in sausage casing and simmered for a few hours. It tastes better than it sounds! "It's a very democratic dish," says Jo Macsween, joint MD of the famous family-run haggis business. "It's a poor man's feast made from humble ingredients that fills you up. It's not about airs and graces which is good symbolism for a man of the earth who rose to meteoric literary fame

**OPPOSITE** Edinburgh's spectacular fireworks display over the Castle is the climax of its Hogmanay celebrations which double the city's population and pump millions into the local economy.

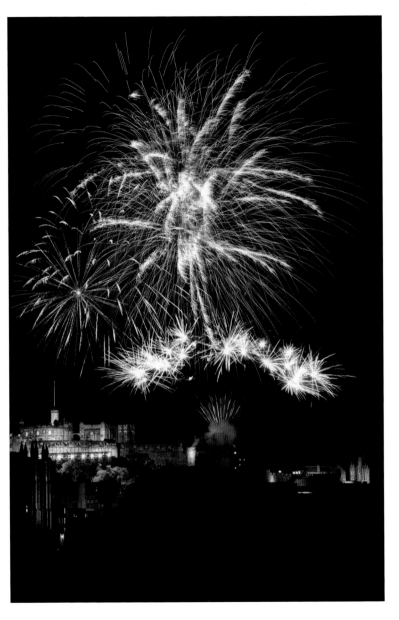

within his own lifetime." Whether or not it was Burns's favourite dish, he clearly enjoyed rubbing the genteel noses of Edinburgh society in those gushing entrails "warm-reekin rich!"

Whisky is the perfect partner not least because its fiery flavours cut through the fat and spice of the dish far better than any wine – a drink that Burns has fun dismissing for its fancy ways in the opening lines of his epic ode to "Scotch Drink": "Let other poets raise a fracas Bout vines, an' wines, an' drucken Bacchus." Yet more than this, the real appeal is the honest, homespun nature of whisky, whose ingredients and origins are every bit as humble as haggis. Admittedly this may have been obscured somewhat by the way Scotch whisky is now priced and promoted, but in Burns's day it was a very earthy spirit indeed. He was certainly fond of a dram, as much for its effect as its taste, as the following line in the same poem makes clear: "But oil'd by thee, the wheels o' life gae down-hill, scrievin, Wi' rattlin glee!"

"Scotch Drink", written in 1785, sees Burns confessing to his muse – good Scots ale and particularly whisky.

---

O Whisky! soul o' plays and pranks!
Accept a bardie's gratfu' thanks!
When wanting thee, what tuneless cranks
Are my poor verses!
Thou comes – they rattle in their ranks,
At ither's arses!

---

The poem continues with a lament for the loss of Ferintosh, Scotland's first true commercial distillery on the Black Isle near Inverness, and then pours scorn on the "curst horse-leeches o' the' Excise". This was somewhat ironic given that Burns became an excise officer four years later in Dumfries. He spent his last eight years in the job, covering large tracts of the county on horse to ensure duty was paid on everything from candles and soap to tea and tobacco. There are no records of him involved with any distillery in the area, though he did apprehend at least one farmer for making moonshine on the side. It also inspired his poem "The De'il's Awa' Wi' th' Exciseman", written in 1792.

The long, damp days in the saddle may have hastened his demise, and Robert Burns died on 21 July 1796, aged 37. His total assets were valued at a mere £200, which scarcely reflects his current value to the Scottish economy. In 2009 the accountant turned comedian Fred MacAuley estimated that "Burns the brand" was worth £160 million a year. He also revealed that the biggest seller by far at the Tam O'Shanter Experience gift shop in Alloway was not the Isle of Arran single malt – the only whisky endorsed by the World Burns Federation. Nor was it postcards, tea-towels or even books of his poems. It was in fact the Rabbie Burns fridge magnet.

The tacky souvenirs may outsell bottles of whisky, but according to one report by an economist at the World Bank in 2003, global sales of Scotch jump 2 per cent on the night, which speaks for itself.

**ABOVE** Rabbie Burns, the national bard, whose self-confessed muse was Scotch, the only drink to wash down some haggis on his 25 January birthday.

**LEFT** Haggis, is traditionally piped in. Having been addressed by the master of ceremonies it is then disembowelled by a sharp knife.

# WHISKY IN POPULAR CULTURE

Sir Harry Lauder was the Billy Connolly of his day, only far more successful. In a forty-year career in vaudeville and music hall, he had become the world's highest-paid performer by 1911 and was the first Scottish artist to sell a million records. According to Sir Winston Churchill he was "Scotland's greatest ever ambassador" – although many Scots might dispute that today, feeling more affinity with Billy Connolly than a sentimental old clown in a kilt.

Born in 1870 in Edinburgh's Portobello, Lauder turned professional in his early twenties and soon had his name in lights above the London Pavilion and other leading music halls. As well as "Roamin' in the Gloamin" and "I Love a Lassie", his hits included "A Wee Deoch an Doris". This is Gaelic for a farewell dram – the sort of drink that leads to another, which is fine so long as you can manage the tongue-twister at the end of the chorus:

Just a wee deoch an doris, just a wee drop, that's all.
Just a wee deoch an doris afore ye gang awa.
There's a wee wifie waitin' in a wee but an ben.
If you can say, "It's a braw bricht moonlicht nicht",
Then yer a'richt, ye ken.

Like his kilt and trademark corkscrew walking stick, Scotch was one of Lauder's props in portraying the comic, drunken Scot – an image that featured in many an Edwardian whisky advert. And, with his 22 tours of America, he may have fostered the idea that if you were not in a kilt, clutching a bottle and swaying gently in the breeze, then you probably weren't Scottish at all. He was knighted for all his fund-raising activities in the First World War, and was close friends with the grocery tycoon Sir Thomas Lipton and the whisky baron Tommy Dewar.

In 1897 Dewar's was the subject of possibly the first

advertising film ever made. Produced by Thomas Edison and associates, it featured four actors who appeared to have raided the dressing-up box for items including a dinner jacket, bearskin, spear and shield. They are all in kilts, one absurdly short, one back to front, and end by dancing a drunken Highland fling in front of a banner for Dewar's White Label. A version for the English market, "Spirit of his Ancestors", was filmed four years later, and had the four kilted men raising a toast to Queen Victoria.

## PROBLEMS WITH PROHIBITION

Before long Scotch whisky was appearing on the big screen, although once Prohibition began, drinking scenes were no longer shown. According to Daniel Okrent in his book *Last Call*, Hollywood initially supported the ban, believing that if people were denied access to the saloon they would flock to the movies. That soon changed, and in a survey of 115 films released in 1929, Okrent found that drinking was depicted in two-thirds of them, "more often than not favourably".

In 1949 London's Ealing Studios released the ultimate whisky film – *Whisky Galore!* – about a Hebridean island community who are saved from a prolonged whisky

LEFT The film *Whisky Galore!* was no sentimental, soft-focus portrayal of Hebridean life during wartime. It was more a riotous celebration of whisky and the islanders' ingenuity at beating the system.

drought by a shipwreck laden with Scotch. Based on Compton Mackenzie's book, which fictionalized the tale of the actual sinking of the SS *Politician* off Eriskay in 1941, the film was directed by Alexander Mackendrick and stars Joan Greenwood, Basil Rathbone, Gordon Jackson and James Robertson Justice. On the eve of its re-release in 2011, *The Independent*'s film critic, Jonathan Romney, wrote that it "stands out as depicting Scottish island culture in a no-nonsense, caricature-free fashion". He added that "modern viewers may be surprised to see how enthusiastically pro-booze *Whisky Galore!* is. It's a celebration of what, the film reminds us, comes from the Gaelic *uisge beatha* – the water of life."

The film was a hit in the States as *Tight Little Island*, and also in France, where its title *Whisky à Go-Go* inspired dozens of whisky bars to spring up. In both countries it fed a real fondness for the land of Scotch. Deluxe blends like Chivas Regal came to symbolize success and status in post-war America, and this image was re-exported by Hollywood to the rest of the world. Visions of glamorous film stars, with a cigarette in one hand and a Scotch in the other, boosted global tobacco and whisky sales no end.

Then came that hard-drinking spy, James Bond. The books by Ian Fleming were laced with whisky, though it was more often bourbon than Scotch, possibly because Fleming's doctor allegedly told him it was healthier than his daily bottle of gin. But when 007 first appeared on screen in *Dr No* in 1962 he brought with him whisky's nemesis – the base of all those "shaken not shtirred" Martinis. The triumph of vodka over whisky is interesting given what was happening in the spirits market at the time. Compared to all the ancestral baggage around Scotch, vodka travelled light as a thoroughly modern spirit like Bond himself.

Whether the films reflected or led these changes, it all came down to money, with Smirnoff prepared to dig deep for its regular guest appearance on screen. Cynics may wonder if today's script writers simply type in "Bond orders a drink" every other scene, with the "drink" auctioned to the highest bidder from the booze industry. In 2012 Scotch made a comeback when some Macallan 50-year-old stars in one brief scene in *Skyfall*. How much its owner, the Edrington Group, paid is a closely guarded secret.

## AWARD-WINNING WHISKY FILM

Far more significant and quite different in tone was *The Angels' Share* by Ken Loach, also released in 2012. As in *Whisky Galore!*, Scotland's national drink takes centre stage in a bittersweet comedy involving bottles of Irn-Bru and a priceless cask of Maltmill – the Islay distillery built within the grounds of Lagavulin.

The distillery operated from 1908 to 1962, though as far as anyone knows its whisky was never bottled as a single malt. The film, written by Paul Laverty and starring first-time actor Paul Brannigan, won the Jury Prize at Cannes. The whisky writer Charlie Maclean was hired as consultant and he played himself in the movie, right down to his monocle and walrus moustache.

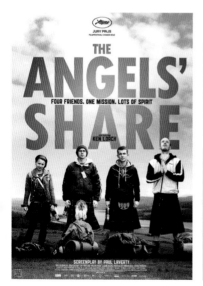

**LEFT** Ken Loach's 2012 whisky heist movie was the first film since *Whisky Galore!* to put Scotch centre stage. It won that year's jury prize at the Cannes film festival.

**BELOW** Few brands exemplified the postwar glamour of Scotch whisky better than the 12 year-old deluxe blend of Chivas Regal.

# WHISKY IN LITERATURE

*"Whiskey to breakfast, whiskey to dinner, whiskey to supper …"* begins a breathless passage in *The Unspeakable Scot*, published in 1902. It continues for a whole paragraph: *"… whiskey when you are well, whiskey if you be sick, whiskey almost as soon as you are born, whiskey the last thing before you die – that is Scotland."* Its English author, T.W.H. Crosland, was laying it on with a trowel because even in 1902 there was more to the country than just whisk(e)y. As for the extra "e", that was fairly common at the time – its use to describe only Irish and American whiskey came later.

There is a long tradition of visitors to Scotland being struck by the natives' fondness for the water of life and its legendary strength, starting with the intrepid explorer, Martin Martin. On reaching the Isle of Lewis at the end of the seventeenth century, he reported on the life-threatening properties of Usquebaugh Baul which was distilled four times. There is no mention of it in Samuel Johnson's *Journey to the Western Isles of Scotland* of 1775, but he did write that: "A man of the Hebrides …, as soon as he appears in the morning, swallows a glass of whisky; yet they are not a drunken race, at least I never was present at much intemperance; but no man is so abstemious as to refuse the morning dram, which they call a skalk."

His companion, James Boswell, added that: "Drinking is in reality an occupation which employs a considerable portion of the time of many people, and to conduct it in the most rational and agreeable manner is one of the great arts of living." Johnson confessed to drinking whisky only once, and found it "preferable to any English malt brandy … [though] what the process was I had no opportunity of enquiring, nor do I wish to improve the art of making poison pleasant".

In *Humphry Clinker*, the picaresque novel of Tobias Smollett published a few years earlier, readers also learned of this mythical spirit "as strong as genever [gin] which they [Highlanders] swallow in great quantities

> Oh, thou demon Drink, thou fell destroyer;
> Thou curse of society, and its greatest annoyer.
> What hast thou done to society, let me think?
> I answer thou hast caused the most of ills, thou demon
> Drink.

without any sign of inebriation. They are used to it from the cradle and find it an excellent preservative against the winter cold, which must be extreme on these mountains." That last point is as true as it ever was.

## SUPPORTERS AND OPPONENTS

Rabbie Burns, writing soon afterwards, had no need to inform his readers what whisky was, and his poems delight in the stuff – more for its effect and what it symbolized [*see page* 172]. A century later the tide was turning, and the incomparable William Topaz McGonagall, teetotal poet and tragedian of Dundee, rose to the challenge with "The Demon Drink":

McGonagall was reflecting the popular press, or least the *Daily Mail*. In a ranting, foam-flecked editorial from 1892, it declared of Edinburgh Old Town that: "not in the

FAR LEFT Like other observers of Scottish life in the eighteenth century, the author Tobias Smollett was struck by how sober people appeared to be despite the impressive volumes of whisky consumed.

LEFT William McGonagall, the famous teetotal bard of Dundee, never doubted his genius. Despite the laughter his recitals provoked, he earnestly believed he should have been poet laureate.

worst dens of New York can a more brutalised crowd be witnessed. Bareheaded and barefooted women with infants in their arms, uncouth Magdalenes scarred with the leprosy of sin, men on the borderland of delirium tremens ..."

Moving forward a few decades to the other side of the pond, Prohibition helped boost spirits like whisky since given the risks of being caught, you may as well be drinking the hard stuff. It also boosted the criminal underworld who now controlled distribution, and gave birth to a new genre of crime fiction. For America's hard-boiled detective – the antithesis of the English gentleman sleuth – beer was a soft drink for pussies. Real men drank Scotch, either in a tumbler relaxing with a broad, or straight from the bottle in its paper bag.

---

**Love makes the world go round? Not at all. Whisky makes it go round twice as fast. That's why I'm the most revolutionary crayture in the whole of Todaidh Mór [*this being Gaelic for the fictional island*]**

---

Among countless tales that sprung from and beyond the era of Prohibition was Raymond Chandler's *Farewell My Lovely* from 1940. In one scene his much-parodied hero, Philip Marlowe, is questioning a suspect: "She poured a fat slug of mellow looking Scotch into my glass, and squirted in some fizz-water. It was the kind of liquor you think you can drink forever, and all you do is get reckless." It was pulp fiction at its finest where whisky was a prop to emphasize the hero's true grit. Caring whether your cocktail was shaken or stirred would have been irredeemably camp. That came later, with a certain spy in the vodka-fuelled adventures of Ian Fleming.

### FACT AND FICTION COME TOGETHER
Before then, Scotch enjoyed its moment of fictional glory in Compton Mackenzie's much-loved *Whisky Galore* in 1947. It was inspired by the true tale of the

wreck of the SS *Politician* off the Hebridean island of
Eriskay. People came from as far as Mull to plunder its
cargo of 28,000 cases of Scotch just like the SS *Cabinet
Minister* in the book. Having worked for MI6 in Syria,
Mackenzie settled on the island of Barra in 1928 and his
affection for the islanders and their ingenuity permeates
*Whisky Galore*. The spirit fuels the community in the
book as the schoolteacher, Norman Macleod, makes
distinctly clear when the island is gripped by a terrible
whisky drought before the wreck.

Whisky swirls in and out of Graham Greene's novels,
notably *The Power and the Glory* (1940) with its flawed
"whisky priest" at the centre. There is also a memorable
scene featuring miniature bottles of Scotch and a game
of draughts in *Our Man in Havana* (1958). While more
recently Scottish crime fiction, or Tartan Noir, is steeped
in the stuff. Whisky trickles through the pages of Ian
Rankin's Inspector Rebus novels, whose hard-drinking
hero was particularly fond of Highland Park.

**BELOW** Raising a dram
to the ill-fated SS
*Politician* which ran
aground here on the
Isle of Eriskay on 5
February 1941 and
inspired Compton
Mackenzie to write the
greatest whisky book of
all. As well as Scotch,
the ship was carrying
a vast and unexplained
stash of Jamaican bank
notes.

# WHISKY TOURISM

When Queen Victoria and Prince Albert first stayed at Balmoral in September 1848, their neighbour, John Begg, who had recently established the Lochnagar distillery next door, invited them round. They duly appeared with various children including the Prince of Wales, then aged seven. Begg later wrote up every detail in his diary, from how they had all sipped his whisky to how he had provoked "a very hearty laugh from Her Majesty". What is amazing, considering the hoops of protocol you would have to go through today, is that Begg's invitation had only been delivered to Balmoral the night before.

From this early peak of whisky tourism, distilleries slipped back into the shadows, and 50 years ago the idea of visiting one while on holiday in Scotland would have seemed bizarre. Distilleries did not advertise their presence and their names were little known beyond the workforce, local residents and the whisky blenders. A few had a tiny following among malt whisky connoisseurs, but most were as anonymous as the big grain distilleries still are. The produce of both types of distillery disappeared almost entirely into blended Scotch.

That began to change with the reinvention of single-malt whisky, starting with Glenfiddich in 1963. Six years later the Speyside distillery opened the first ever distillery visitors' centre. Plenty in the industry were sceptical that anyone would want to visit a "factory" while touring the Highlands, but they were wrong. As James Sugden OBE, the former MD of Johnstons of Elgin, the famous textile company, put it: "It's like *Charlie and the Chocolate Factory*. People on holiday want to see other people at work."

As other malt distilleries began laying down stocks to release their own single malts, they realized there was a real interest in provenance among whisky drinkers. It was enough to say "bottled in Scotland" on the label of blended Scotch, but with malts people were curious to learn more. Disused malt barns and floor maltings were converted into visitor centres and shops, as travel companies added distilleries to their list of castles, gardens and battlefields to visit on their bus tours of Scotland. By 2011 some 52 distilleries, almost half the total, were officially open to the public and attracting 1.3 million visitors a year. Meanwhile the rest were drawing a dedicated band of "whisky anoraks" who traipsed around the country bagging far-flung distilleries as others bag Munros (Scottish peaks over 3,000 ft). The more inaccessible and officially closed to visitors they were, the better.

## SPREADING THE WORD

As "Scotland in a bottle" Scotch whisky has always helped attract visitors to the country. Single malts have inspired them to delve deeper and discover the source. And, unlike visiting a winery that only springs into life for a few weeks during the harvest, whisky making is a year-round process. It is hard not to be seduced if you experience it in the flesh and see and smell the washbacks fermenting, followed by the sweet scent of spirit radiating from gleaming copper stills. To welcome visitors, show them round and serve them in the

**BELOW** Queen Victoria and Prince Albert picnicking near Balmoral in 1861. Thirteen years earlier they had been among the first whisky tourists in history when they visited the neighbouring distillery of Lochnagar. It was soon calling itself Royal Lochnagar.

distillery shop and café there are now around 650 people employed in whisky tourism in Scotland. In direct terms it may not be a hugely profitable enterprise for the distillers, but if it helps recruit loyal disciples in distant markets who will then spread the word, its benefits are immeasurable.

Two well-known blends have followed the same path, starting with Dewar's World of Whisky which sprung up in 2000 beside the brand's spiritual home – the Aberfeldy distillery in Perthshire. With all its archive material and interactive displays, it plays homage to one of the founding fathers of the brand, Tommy Dewar. Two years later and not far away, the tiny Glenturret distillery near Crieff was transformed into The Famous Grouse Experience. It now claims to be one of the top three whisky visitor attractions in the world, but as with Dewar's World of Whisky it can be easy to forget there is actually a malt distillery buried beneath all the heavy branding.

### THE SCOTCH WHISKY HERITAGE CENTRE

Before the blends got in on the act, the whisky industry realized it needed some kind of embassy in Edinburgh

**RIGHT** Blends have joined the whisky tourism trail, with Dewar's World of Whisky at Aberfeldy distillery in Perthshire in 2000.

where people could come and learn about Scotch whisky without having to visit an actual distillery. The nearest, Glenkinchie, is half an hour from the city centre and not so easy to visit without your own car. In 1987, 19 whisky companies invested £2 million each to acquire an abandoned primary school and convert it into the Scotch Whisky Heritage Centre. Right next to Edinburgh Castle, it could hardly have had a better location.

From 70,000 visitors the first year, the Heritage Centre was attracting over a quarter of a million by 2009 when it was given a £3 million face-lift. The highlight of the tour is a Disney-like barrel ride through the whisky-making process. To quote the official description, you will be taken from "gently-swaying fields of barley" past the "steaming and bubbling Pot Still", and finally to the "tick-tock of the passing years of maturation". The tour ends with the world's largest collection of Scotch whisky, some 3,384 bottles amassed by the Brazilian collector Claive Vidiz and bought by Diageo for an undisclosed sum in 2008.

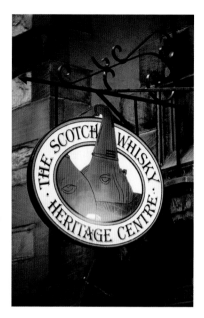

ABOVE A stone's throw from Edinburgh Castle, the Scotch Whisky Heritage Centre acts as an embassy for the industry, attracting thousands who don't have the time or inclination to visit an actual distillery.

## GLASGOW'S OWN

Five years later plans for a similar venture were unveiled for Glasgow, though with a crucial difference. Housed in the old pump house of the Queen's Dock on the Clyde, the Glasgow Distillery Company will produce its own whisky. It will be the first new distillery in the city for over a hundred years, and is the brainchild of Tim Morrison, whose family used to own Morrison Bowmore. Once up and running its still-room will be filled with sweet spirity aromas, making it far more than just another heritage centre.

# INDEX

# CREDITS

## PICTURE CREDITS

The publishers would like to thank the following sources for their kind permission to reproduce the pictures in this book.

**The Advertising Archives:** 158
**Alamy:** /Bildagentur-online Historical Collection: 24; /John Bracegirdle: 126; / Richard Broadwell: 185; /Chronicle: 33B; / Mark Collinson: 128; /Derek Croucher: 148; / Stephen Finn: 94; /David Harding: 46-47; / Dennis Hardley: 75L; /Jan Holm: 146; /Peter Horree: 40; /Catherine Karnow/Corbis Flirt: 142; /Elizabeth Leyden: 156; /Lphoto: 184; /Mirrorpix: 132; /Jose Antonio Moreno Castellano/imageBROKER: 80; /David Osborn: 100, 113, 114; /John Peter Photography: 139T; /Photos 12: 177L; /Klaus Rainer Krieger/imageBROKER: 53; / Reuters: 137; /David Robertson: 56; /Scottish Viewpoint: 140, 152; /John Short/Vantage: 42; /Dave Tacon: 124; /travelib: 23; /S Vannini/De Agostini/UIG: 144; /Alan Wilson: 16R
**Auchentoshan:** 164, 165, 166
**Bridgeman Images:** /Historic England: 19; / Universal History Archive/UIG: 18
**Bruichladdich:** 61, 62, 63
**Burn Stewart:** 83
**Campari Group:** 9, 44, 133, 134T, 134B
**Depositphotos:** 107B
**Diageo:** 76, 79, 136L, 136R, 160, 161, 162
**Edrington Group:** 99
**Getty Images:** /Mary Ann Anderson/MCT: 90; /Craig Barritt: 117; /Bettmann: 6, 26, 28, 36; /Margaret Bourke-White/The Life Picture Collection: 34; /Simon Butterworth: 78; /Alan Copson: 48; /Simon Dawson/ Bloomberg: 3, 4; /Evening Standard: 173B; / Rocco Fasano: 45; /Garrett M Graff/MCT: 89; /Tim Graham: 72, 82; /Mark Hamblin: 168-169; /History of Advertising Trust/ Heritage Images: 119T; /Hulton Archive: 32; /

John Lawson/Belhaven Moment: 102; /Matt Mawson/Corbis Documentary: 121; /Jeff J Mitchell: 106; /Steven Morris Photography: 70; /MyLoupe/UIG: 77; /NY Daily News: 39L; /Peter Ribbeck: 84; /Will Robb: 58; / Pete Rowbottom: 111; /Stock Montage: 173T; /Jeremy Sutton-Hibbert: 96; /TCI/EyeOn/ UIG: 12-13, 122; /Charles Twist: 81; /UIG: 31R, 69, 108; /Sandro Vannini/Corbis Documentary: 41, 125; /VisitBritain/Britain on View: 54
**Glenfarclas:** 143
**Glenfiddich:** 9
**Glenlivet:** 119B
**Glenrothes:** 129, 130
**Harris Distillery:** 75R
**The Irish Historical Picture Company:** 31L
**iStockphoto:** 153, 191
**Laphroaig:** 65L, 66, 67
**Mary Evans:** 65R, 179R, 183; /Grosvenor Prints: 16L
**Morrison Bowmore:** 167
**Old Pulteney:** 87, 93
**Pernod Ricard:** 116
**Private Collections:** 33T, 55, 59, 71, 91, 95, 103, 115, 123, 127, 131, 135, 139B, 147, 163
**REX/Shutterstock:** /Jim Hutchison/ Associated Newspapers: 181; /Studio Canal: 39R, 175
**Shutterstock:** 98, 105, 107T, 141, 145, 150, 171, 177R
**Springbank:** 155
**Topfoto:** 29T, 37, 118, 179L; /Barnes: 14; /City of London/HIP: 22; /Land Lost Content/ HIP: 29B
**Wikimedia Commons:** 15, 21

Every effort has been made to acknowledge correctly and contact the source and/or copyright holder of each picture and Carlton Books Limited apologises for any unintentional errors or omissions that will be corrected in future editions of this book.

## PUBLISHERS' ACKNOWLEDGMENTS

The Publishers would like to thank the following people and organisations for their help in providing information, images and other material for this book: Christine McCafferty at Diageo plc; Alison Morris and Eleanor Kidd at Elgin Library and Moray Council Archives; Jim Long and Chris Brousseau at the Chivas Brothers' Archive and Pernod-Ricard; Alice at Mail Marketing (Scotland) Ltd on behalf of Laphroaig; The National Library of Scotland; and Dr Stephanie Metze and Tessa Spencer at the National Records of Scotland.